AF556358

HUMAN RESOURCE ACCOUNTING

HUMAN RESOURCE ACCOUNTING

With Special Reference to Charitable Institutions

Malayendu Saha

DISCOVERY PUBLISHING HOUSE
NEW DELHI - 110002 (INDIA)

First Published - 1997

Reprinted-2011

ISBN 81-7141-346-3

Published by :

Discovery Publishing House
4831/24, Ansari Road, Darya Ganj,
New Delhi - 110 002 (INDIA)
Phone : 327 9245
Fax. : 91-11-3253475

Laser Typesetting by :

Debug Computer Services
Delhi.

Mehra Offset Press
Delhi

Dedicated To My Parents

LATE MANMATHA SAHA

AND

MRS. RANU SAHA

Whose blessings are my fountain of inspiration

Contents

Foreword

Of the present books on accounting for a non-profit organisation — purely analytical, procedural, descriptive or prescriptive — there are a great number. Of books on accounting for human resources of profit-seeking organisations — valuation principles, disclosures methods and reporting systems — there is an equal profusion. To my knowledge, however, Dr. Saha is breaking entirely new ground in developing the whole of his work around a discussion of an accounting system where the services rendered to the people by non-profit organisations as well as the value of the selfless people providing these services and who are the fountain of such services can be measured and reported.

The conventional system of accounting for non-profit organisations is confined to reflecting how far the restrictions imposed by resources providers are adhered to. It can neither present the value of the services the non-profit organisations provide, nor reflect the value of the resources of these services.

This book makes a radical departure from the conventional perceptive. Since the objective of an accounting system should be reporting the performance of an entity in terms of its goals, Dr. Saha has aptly tried to devise a system which can help reflect the value of the services rendered by the non-profit organisations, in general, and the charitable institutions in particular. He has also designed an accounting system to measure the value of the sources of such services, that is, the value of the people who are committed to serve the society.

Consequently, it is an ideal book for researchers interested in measuring and reporting of services rendered by non-profit organisations. Moreover, this book is of immense help to practitioners, whose primary task is to find out the means of presenting, in an objective manner, the value of benevolent services of the people of the charitable institutions. It might also be of interest to teachers and students at postgraduate level by providing a straightforward and detailed introduction to the subject. In addition, accounting policy-makers responsible for formulating accounting policies, funding agencies interested in the effective functioning of non-profit organisations, as well as those who represent public interest, would find this book beneficial.

Dr. G. C. Sinha
Professor,
Department of Commerce,
University of Calcutta.

Preface

During the recent past, the accounting scenario across the world has undergone substantial changes. With the advancement and modernisation in the concept and techniques of accounting, there arises constant demand to bring new dimensions of financial reporting by entities. Various organisations, in recent times, in their published accounts annex a supplementary report embracing Human Resource Accounting, Social Accounting, Value Added Statement etc,. Thus, inclusion of new concepts in the financial reports not only provide more logical and efficient decisions and control. However, whatever developments in the accounting concepts have been made they are basically restricted to application in the profit seeking organisations only. Neither any urgency has been felt in applying these new concepts in non-profit seeking organisations, nor does anybody think about developments in the accounting and financial reporting practices of the non-profit entities.

The accounting for non-profit organisations is based on the principles of conventional accounting system and represent the sources from which various funds are generated and the avenues they are expended during a particular accounting period. But it does not provide any information on their service potentiality nor makes any attempt for valuation of the human resources associated with the entity. The present volume, is designed to fill the vacuum to some extent and to provide further discussion in the field.

It may be mentioned that this book is a modified version of the author's doctoral thesis which earned him the degree of Ph.D. of the University of Calcutta. The thesis was prepared under the supervision and guidance of Prof. G.C. Sinha, Dean and Head of the faculty of Business Studies, University of Calcutta. The idea of the work originally sprang up out of lively discussion with him about the necessity of reporting the sacrifices of the selfless people associated with the welfare organisations.

I would like to acknowledge my indebtedness to my researchmentor Prof. Sinha for his wise and valuable guidance, and the mental support required to undertake the tedious assignment.

I am also extremely grateful to the teachers of the Department of Commerce and Business Management, University of Calcutta, for their valuable opinions and suggestions in connection with my study.

I also extend my gratitude to the former Chairperson of the Government and Nonprofit Section of the American Accounting Association, Prof. Jesse W Huges, Department of Accountancy, Old Dominion University, Norfolk, USA, for his cogitative notions which are annexed for the development of the Volume. I also wish to acknowledge the invaluable assistance provided by Prof. Earl Wilson, School of Accounting, University of Missouri, Columbia, and Prof. W.T. Wrege, Department of Accounting, Ball State University, Muncie, in terms of furnishing me with necessary literatures free of cost.

I am also immensely indebted to the learned authors of India and abroad for the help that I took from their works.

Thanks are due to my wife, Papiya, for her untiring secretarial work and constant courage in connection with this edition and to my son, Rohit, for many of his lost hours of his covetable association with me.

Malayendu Saha

1

Introduction

The Issue

One of the major purposes of annual financial reporting, particularly for not-for-profit organization, is to provide information for evaluating the effectiveness of the management of resources in achieving organization's goals. Again, " performance measures should be quantified in terms of Identified goals".[1] In case of business organizations the basic objective is to earn profit through employing resources, while in case of nonprofit organizations like charitable institutions, the primary objective is to provide services through the effective use of resources provided by the funding agencies. Profits earned and the services rendered are the outcome of the effective utilisation of the resources employed for the purpose. Accounting aims to report them periodically. Hence, to have a clear idea about how much of the objective of an organization has been achieved requires a precise but important information on both profits earned or services rendered and resources utilised for the purpose. Income Statements and Balance Sheets are designed to reflect the annual earnings and resources position at the year end. It is generally inferred that income is the outcome of resources. In other words, income is the flow and resources are the sources of such flow.[2] Which is why, through calculating return on investment (ROI) we can derive the rate of return on such resources. Usually land and building, plant and machinery, inventories and monetary claims are traditionally considered as resources. But they themselves cannot generate goods or services. It is men with the help of whom these assess can be operated. In fact, they are the catalysts of the production process. More the efficient the employees, more the rate of earning. Paradoxically, value of such human resources (HRs) are not conventionally reported in our financial statements. Even the expenses incurred for the selection, recruitment and training with a view to acquiring and developing such resources for deriving services from them are neither capitalised nor amortized in the books of accounts. That is why developed the concept of human resource accounting (HRA). In absence of reporting the value of these HRs the complete financial picture of profit earning and the sources of such earnings of a profit seeking organization is not available.

The problem is aggravated further in case of nonprofit organization (NPOs)[3], where the primary objective, it is mentioned earlier, is to render services to the society with the help of resources used for the purpose. The basic objective of reporting here should be providing information on the services rendered by it and its efficiency and effectiveness in providing these services.[4] Measurement of effective use depends on two factors : one, services rendered and two, resources used for the purpose. The present accounting system does not make provision for supplying complete information on both of the two. Here services are not measure and resources engaged in generating the services are not fully reported. In fact, in a NPO, some people come together, collect some donations and volunteer their labour to render services usually at free of charges [5] or at a minimum rate to the members of the society. The resources available here through donations, contributions etc. is not of primary considerations. These people associated with these entities volunteer their services usually benevolently or in exchange of a token salary. The magnitude of services which a NPO provides , depends on the generosity of these people. That apart, in case of profit seeking organizations, an argument though not so plausible, may be given in support of non-disclosure of the value of Hrs. Existing set of employees may be easily replaced by another without incurring heavy expenses, and without compromising considerably the primary objective of earning profit. It is so because, in perfect competition the marginal revenue available from the services of an employee is assumed to be equal to wages payable to him. But this argument does not hold good for a NPO, in general, and for charitable institution, in particular where the basic objective is to generate and distribute services to the weaker section of the society. Moreover, in such cases, the role of its physical and monetary assets in relation to its associated people is very insignificant. The basic objective of providing services cannot be fulfilled without the wholehearted labour of the people associated with the NPOs. That is why reporting of the values of HRs is of much significance in case of NPOs. But the conventional accounting system makes provisions neither to report the value of services derived from them, nor the information on the value of those human resources. The traditional system usually aims to reflect how far the restrictions imposed by the resource providers are adhered to[6]. Hence, it appears that the objective (of financial reporting of a NPO) of reporting the services rendered by it and its effectiveness in the use of resources is not fulfilled to a considerable extent.

With a view to bridging the gap between what is expected of accounting system of a NPO and what is actually provided by the conventional accounting practices in this area, the services rendered by the organization should be valued and reported. Moreover, the value of human resources, the primary source of such services, should also be accounted for. Services rendered to society by NPO, in fact, flow mainly from HRs. Measurement of a flow cannot be completed unless its origin or source is accounted for. The traditional accounting system of NPO makes provision for measuring and reporting neither the flow of these services nor the stock or sources of such services. The present study is an humble approach to find out a solution, if possible.

I

The Objective of the Study

Machines and materials together in an organization can produce nothing without help from human hands. The greater the efficiency of the Human forces, the greater the profit earning capacity of a firm. Generally, the performance of an organization depends very much on the behaviour of the human forces it acquires. But that is not reflected in the conventional accounts. The situation is more serious in case of NPOs. While the ultimate goal of the profit organization is to earn profit for individuals,[7] the objective of NPOs is to provide social services without any intention of realising profit.[8] Thus, generation and distribution of services rather than earning of profit is the primary objective of the NPOs. Here, the services rendered and sacrifices made by HRs are far more important than expenses made on office and administration. It is so because they are set up with the basic objective of providing services to the society through their personnel who volunteer their labour for the cause of the society. For instance, Rama Krishna Mission, Bharat Sevasharam Sangha and similar other Voluntary and Welfare organizations in India have been set up with the basic objective of providing services to the poor usually at free of cost.

Therefore, the objective of accounting of NPOs should not be to measure how much physical wealth is at their disposal; rather it should extend to reporting the services rendered by the personnel in the organization who have dedicated their lives for the cause and betterment of the mankind. In fact, the latter should be given precedence to the former. It is also worthmentioning here that, there are various types of organizations like governments, local self governments, voluntary organizations, clubs, hospitals etc. which are established with the objective of rendering social services rather than earning profit. The accounting system of all of them, however, are not identical. Of course, there is one thing in common among them. In all cases, the objective is to report whether the funds entrusted to these entities, are utilised according to the restrictions imposed on them by the funding agencies or resource providers. That is why, respective accounting frameworks have been geared to what is popularly called, "Fund Accounting".[9] Here the principal objective of accounting is to guard against any probable fraud and misappropriation of funds. Even though the present system is capable of accomplishing their objectives, it fails to show how efficiently the resources are utilised. Here neither return of capital, nor return on capital should be the basic thing to be reported. On the contrary, the information on the quantum of the services expected to be derived from the people involved in the entity can serve the donors better in their decisions as to the amount they will contribute in future. Hence, the role of HRs, in comparison to other assets in NPOs is far greater than that in POs. The other important point is that, so far as this author's knowledge goes, none of the institutions reports in their financial statements on the value of HRs employed in those organizations.

The present study attempts to study the accounting system of one category of NPOs, namely the charitable institutions, and tries to account for the HRs involved in organization. Hence, the objective of the study may be summed up as follows :

(i) To measure the values of HRs engaged in a NPO.

(ii) To examine the position of the value of HRs in relation to other assets in a NPO.

(iii) To Highlight the contributions to society made by the dedicated people of the organization.

(iv) To evolve an index of performance of a NPO in terms of accounting indicators.

(v) To estimate the relative contributions to the society made by the funding agencies and the people serving the NPO, and ultimately,

(vi) To devise a system of accounting for a NPO, so that the extent to which the basic objective of the Organization for which it is meant for can be presented in the annual accounting statements.

II

Research Methodology

The whole exercise accomplished in this study is more or less conceptual. The study neither aims to develop a new theory of HRA nor aspires to modify what has been previously known on the subject. It has attempted to apply to a NPO a popular HRA model which is usually applied to POs.

Since the inquiry basically aims to apply HRA models to NPOs, the study has restored to a two-pronged approach in solving the problem. On the one hand, it has made a discussion at the theoretical level on the development of major HRA models, their relative merits and demerits and the problems involved in measuring the value of HRs as per the models. An accounting model has also been suggested to reflect the accomplishment of the objectives of the NPO for which it is set up. On the other, an attempt has been made to apply one important HRA model, the application of which seems feasible. With a view to have an empirical verification of the model, a NPO has been selected for our study.

The Rama Krishna Mission Hospital and charitable unit, both under the supervision of Rama Krishna Boys' Home, Rahara North 24-Parganas, West Bengal, India, are considered for our study. The financial reports of the organization are considered and through administering questionnaire various bits of information are collected for human resource accounting. Then an attempt has been made to integrate the financial report and the HRA according to the proposed accounting model. For the purpose a comparative analysis between the present and the proposed accounting system is made through some accounting ratios based on the proposed accounting statement. Lastly, an attempt has been made to highlight how the proposed accounting system can supplement the existing system to portray the achievements of the basic objectives of a NPO for which the same has been set up.

III

The Scheme of Work

The work comprises of seven chapters. *Chapter One*, by way of introduction, endeavours to highlight the various problems which are not encountered by the conventional accounting practices in NPOs. The objective of the present study, the research methodology and the scheme of work are also discussed in this chapter. While the following five chapters are engrossed in the conceptual discussions and empirical verification on HRA in NPOs, the last one is engaged in concluding the study.

Since the enquiry basically aims to account for HRs of NPOs, the study comprises of conceptual discussion supported by empirical verifications. Having considered the historical developments of the concepts on HRA, *Chapter Two* has briefly presented by the major HRA models enunciated by various authorities and ultimately has selected one of them which appears to be appropriate for empirical study in the present context.

Chapter Three makes an attempt to analyse the various aspects of NPOs. In doing so, it examines the features of these organizations, studies their impact on accounting practices, highlights the existing objectives of accounting of such organizations and compares between conventional accounting principles of NPOs and the POs and presents an outline of the existing practices in NPOs.

The question that whether or not the existing accounting system of NPOs is geared up to provide sufficient and useful information according to their objectives, has been thrashed out in *Chapter Four*. It attempts to develop an accounting model which may supplement the existing accounting system of NPOs to provide necessary information in respect of the services rendered by the employees, the contributors and also by the organization itself. This is for identifying how much of the objectives for which NPOs have been established has been achieved.

The accounting model, as proposed in the previous section requires empirical verification. It has been applied to a NPO, namely, the Rama Krishna Mission Boys' Home, Rahara. The hospital and charitable unit run by the organization is the object of our study. *Chapter Five* thrives for applying the model to the above charitable unit to test the outcome of the model.

After considering the conceptual aspects of accounting framework of NPOs, the study attempts to value the services of the dedicated personnel. *Chapter Six* seeks to measure the value of these HRs based on the model proposed by Baruch Lev and Aba Schwartz, since this model is widely accepted. In recent days this method of valuing HRs is considered appropriate by the POs.

By way of summarising what has been done in the earlier chapters, the last one i.e. *Chapter Seven* is engrossed in concluding how the proposed model will act as a supplement to the existing system with a view to indicating how far the basic objective for which the NPOs are established has been achieved. It also points out some related areas where further investigation is warranted.

References

1. FASB, Trueblood Report : Objective No. 11, as reported in Ahmed Belkaoui, *Accounting Theory*, Harcourt Brace, Jovanovich International Edition, Washington, 1985, p. 179.

2. E.S. Hendriksen, *Accounting Theory*, Richard. D. Irwin, 3rd Edition, 1977, p. 145.

3. Nonprofit organizations range from large and complex to the small and simple ones. They include hospitals, colleges and universities, religious organizations, associations, foundations, cultural institutions and the voluntary social service organizations. The features of the nonprofit organizations have been discussed in detail in Chapter-III. Voluntary social service organizations are selected for our study, since in this area whole hearted involvement of HRs is indispensable for achieving the objective of such organizations.

4. Statement of Financial Accounting Concepts (SFAC) No. 4 - "Objectives of Financial Reporting by Nonbusiness Organizations", *Journal of Accountancy* (Paragraph - 30) March 1981, p. 117.

5. Statement of Financial Accounting Concepts No. : 4 - "Objectives of Financial Reporting by Nonbusiness Organizations", *Journal of Accountancy*, (Paragraph 17), March 1981, p. 115.

6. Statement of Financial Accounting Concept No. 4 - "Objective of Financial Reporting by Nonbusiness Organizations", *Journal of Accountancy*, March 1981, P-113.

7. R. Ruggels & N. Ruggels, *National Income Accounts and Income Analysis*, McGraw-Hill Book Co. 1949, p. 9.

8. Emerson O. Henke, *Introduction to Nonprofit Organization Accounting*, PWS-KENT Publishing Co., (3rd Edition), 1988, p. 2.

9. William Warshauer Jr., Malvern J. Gross, Jr. and Joel W. Meyerson, "Nonprofit Enterprises", *Acountants' Handbook*, (Vol. 2, 6th Edition) edited by Lee J. Seidler, D.R. Carmichael, A Ronald Press Publication, 1981, Section - 43.

2

Concepts and Techniques of Human Resource Accounting and their Application

Introduction

Valuation of HRs associated with NPOs requires a survey of literature on the measurement of the resources, needs a comparative analysis of the various models and demands selection of one of them which is most suitable in the context of availability of data and other considerations. HRs, it has been stated earlier, represent the heart and brain of organization. For the last few decades, the accounting scenario across the world is much concerned with the valuation of human resources and reporting the same in the annual accounting statements. The accounting scholars are also deeply engrossed in the subject, even though they do not agree in all aspects in the area. This chapter aims to survey, in brief, the major conceptual developments on this issue.

With the object of surveying the ideas developed in the area the present chapter delineates first, what is usually meant by human resource accounting (HRA) and inquires the rationale behind such system of accounting. The crux of the problem of HRA, i.e. the measurement of the value of HRs in an organization is narrated in section three. Subsequently it highlights the early writings and presents also the historical evolution made on this subject. Next to it, a detailed analysis is made on the various models developed by the erudite authorities, followed by a comparative discussion on those issues. An appraisal of these models, leads us to confine our study to one of the most widely accepted theories, the application of which is feasible in measuring the value of HRs in NPOs. How the human assets are reflected by profit-seeking organizations in India in their annual reports is discussed in section nine while a bird's view on the recent practices made by some major organizations in India reporting HRA is shown in section ten. By way of conclusion the chapter discusses the need for accounting for HRs of the NPOs and for valuing the services of the people associated with these organizations.

I

Major Definitions HRA

Now discussion on some major definitions of HRA are in order.

The Committee on HRA of American Accounting Association (AAA) defines HRA as "the process of identifying and measuring data about human resources and communicating this information to interested parties"[1].

According to Davidson *et al*, HRA is, "a term used to describe a variety of proposals that seeks to report and emphasize the importance of human resources - knowledgeable, trained and loyal employees - in a company's earning process and total assets"[2].

Flamholtz defines HRA as "accounting for people as an organizational resource. It involves measuring the costs incurred by business firms and other organizations to recruit, select, hire, train and develop human assets. It also involves measuring the economic value of people to organizations"[3].

Brummet explains HRA as, "the process of developing financial assessments for people within organization and society and the monitoring of these assessments through time. It deals with investments in people and with economic results of those investments"[4].

An observation on the above definitions leads us to the conclusion that accounting for HRs involves the following process, viz:

(i) identification of data on the investment on human resources ;

(ii) measurement and valuation of the economic results of such investments, and

(iii) presentation of the above valuations in the annual financial statements.

While the expenditure incurred for recruiting and developing personnel in an organization is considered by some authorities as investment in HRs, the present values of the series of services derivable from such resources are treated by others as the value of such resources. Anyway, all agree on the point that information on the above is to be provided in the financial statements to make the accounting reporting complete and useful.

II

Needs for HRA

HRs are indispensable components of an organization. They represent the people of all levels engaged within an entity. The inanimate objects alone in an organization can produce nothing without the help from HRs. The success of an organization hangs ultimately on the efficiency of its HRs. Hence the objectives of an organization should, therefore, be to acquire their services, to develop their skill, to motivate the people to enhance their level of performance and ultimately to ensure that they continue to maintain their commitment to the organization. These operations are performed by all the organizations, whether they are profit-seeking or non-profit seeking to achieve their desired objectives.

With the increasing sizes and complexities of business units, advancement in the economic role of the governments, the emergence of scientific management within the organization and development in the accounting techniques necessitate to bring new dimensions in accounting for a vital element of the resources - man. Recently, the top level management is very much concerned with the ideas : What is the impact of inclusion of HRs in the financial statements ? Can the performance of these HRs be measured and shown in the Balance Sheet ? What purposes these financial reports will serve if the HRs find a place in the annual accounting statement ? In this section will be discussed in brief the necessity of HRA in an organization.

(i) **Providing complete picture :** The conventional accounting system is, however silent on the concept of HRA. According to this system, the expenses incurred for the selection, recruitment, training etc. are considered as current revenue expenses rather than an investment for the purpose of being amortized over its useful economic service life. As a result, the conventional balance sheets fail to represent the value of HRs and hence these financial reports are unable to reflect the true value of the enterprises and the rate of return on actual investments[5]. The ROI, in such circumstances, shows a brighter image than what is the actual position. This is why information on HRs is necessary to provide a complete picture of the assets-holding of an organization.

(ii) **Control :** Data derived from HRA can be used as a tool in the hands of management for effective control of the organization. According to Flamholtz, HRA generally provides information essential for management to perform the functions of acquiring, developing, allocating, conserving, utilising, evaluating and rewarding HRs[6]. The result so achieved through using HRA for reporting may also be of crucial significance in the management control system.[7]

(iii) **Information to others :** The other users of the financial reports may also be benefitted through the publication of HRA information. Some authorities opine in favour of HRA. In the opinion of Rensis Likert, "Bankers making loans, investment house and others, who are interested in the earnings and success of the enterprise, should be just as interested as Board of Directors and senior officers in having these periodic measurement of the causal and intervening variables"[8]. Where the causal variables denote the strategy, skill and policies of leadership, the intervening variables reflect internal health, state and performance capabilities of the organizations. Hermanson contemplated that the financial statements would be more complete and more useful to managers and investors if they include in their accounting reporting the value of those HRs who served the entity[9].

(iv) **Information on efficiency of HRs :** Investors' need for HRA information, for they feel that an entity with skilled, efficient and wise HRs is more desirable for investment, as they may get higher rate of capital gains from their securities and expect greater service potentials than from those with inefficient working force. As per the report of

American Accounting Association (Committee on Human Resource Accounting) the purpose of HRA is to improve the quality of decision making by external users, particularly the investors, who could benefit from HRA through the provision of information on the extent to which the human assets of the organization have been increased, or have diminished during the period[10]. Moreover, the efficiency of HRs can also be measured through the HRA.

(v) **Indicator of prospective profits :** The human-assets investment ratio (i.e. the ratio of investment in human resources to total assets) may be regarded as a very useful tool to indicate the relative position of HRs in relation to other assets of the organization and also serve as an important indicator of future profit performance to the investors and other interested parties.[11]

(vi) **Provides information on non-monetary attributes :** The users would be served better if non-monetary attributes are presented in the annual reports. It is so, because, measurement of services and reporting of such non-monetary attributes will make the information system more logical and authentic. In case of NPOs, where HRs are the most important elements of the organisations, information on them in the financial statement is very much essential to highlight their performances. As Eric Flamholtz opines, "HRA would first, identify the variables which determine a person's value to an organization that would suggest in developing monetary measures of human value and second, by identifying the variables the theory would facilitate the development of non-monetary surrogate measures of human value."[12]

(vii) **Helps developing employee behaviour :** Management may also be benefited from the information on their human resources in their financial statement as it would result in developing employees behaviour and skill, monitoring their efficiency of performance, lowering turnover and absenteeism and improving the human relation.[13] The HRs, when placed in the Balance Sheet as assets of the organization, may achieve some psychological impetus, which ultimately influence their performance in the organization.

(viii) **Helps making comparative analysis :** Comparison of performance between monetary and non-monetary attributes is of immense help to the management for efficient control of the organization. A number of ratios may be suggested for such comparison. A number of ratios may be suggested for such comparison. Baruch Lev and Aba Schwartz have opined in favour of such ratio analysis and have suggested a set of financial ratios. They are : (i) ratio of human to non-human capital (labour intensity), (ii) ratio of the value of scientific staff to the total value of human capital (skill intensity).[14] These ratios will, in fact, determine the value of HRs in comparison to the total assets of the organization and ultimately measure their performance within the organization.

(ix) **Helps in making decisions :** The information on HRs in financial statement and the changes in the value of HR assets over time are important to the interested people for making decisions and choosing among alternatives. The resource providers may decide on their proposed investment on the basis of the rate of return of the entity. A firm, incorporating HRs in their financial statements, will present more accurate rate of return on investment than a firm which fails to include HRs in their accounting reporting.

(x) **Helps in determining profitability and productivity :** The funding agencies of the profit seeking organization are very much concerned with the firm's profitability which is the function of the productivity of HRs associated with it. That is why the HRs should be shown as assets in the financial statement to give a meaningful and comparable measure of productivity. The profitability, on the other hand, presents the performance and credit-worthiness of an entity and such information can only be portrayed by incorporating the value of both human and non-human assets in financial statements.

(xi) **Helps in efficient utilisation of human resources :** HRA also helps the management in utilising the human resources in the most effective and efficient manner and ultimately stipulating a conceptual framework on the acquisition, development, allocation, conservation, designed to influence the value of the people.[15]

Thus, it is evident from the above discussions that, to provide a more realistic financial picture of an organization it is the financial statements which will ensure more comparability and completeness of accounting reporting. Thus it provides more useful information as an aid to financial analysis.

III

Hurdles to the Introduction of HRA to An Organization

Adoption of HRA system helps in deriving some advantages, but some hurdles are to be overcome for the same. Some of the hurdles are listed below :

1. A number of models have been developed for the valuation of HRs of an organization, but it is difficult to collect data to fit the models. That apart, the authoritative bodies do not recommend for the introduction of a specific model. Which is why no uniform principle or standard is established for the measurement of such resources.

2. The management are least interested in the valuation of HRs on the following grounds :

   (a) The valuation models are very complex to comprehend and implement ;

   (b) Most of them are least interested in highlighting the value of their subordinates ;

   (c) There is no legal compulsion for disclosing the same in the accounting reports ;

   (d) Introduction of the system does not entitle an organization tax relief on the expenses on HR development programmes.

3 The investors as well as the management of the profit-seeking organizations are interested in the magnitude of profit earned by the entity. The system of HRA, in fact, neither assist in enhancing the profit structure, nor helps in presenting the financial data in brighter way.

4. Since the values are based on estimates rather than on exchanges, the resultant statements are sometimes considered subjective, surmise and imaginative.

5. Moreover, as discussed earlier, something can be considered as asset if it is owned by the entity. As no ownership can be claimed on HRs, they cannot be sold in need. Most of the people concerned are, therefore, reluctant to measure and report such resources in the financial statements.

These limitations notwithstanding, it can be claimed that HRA opens new vistas in the accounting world so that there will be a scope for evaluating and reporting HRs associated with an entity.

IV

Evolution of Human Resources Accounting

Since long past, authorities considered the HRs indispensable in an organization. But the concept of accounting for the services of those HRs of the organization did not take a concrete form in early writings. Adam Smith, for instance, contemplated the investment in human capital.

Alfred Marshall also mentioned that "the most valuable of all capital is that invested in human beings."[16] But a major breakthrough was not made in those days.

Subsequently in the post World war period, scholars like T. W. Schultz, Gary Becker, E. F. Dennison, L. Throw deliberated vigorously on the concept of human capital.

The Conventional accounting system, it is discussed earlier, generally reflects the information on uses, utilities and values of inanimate objects without portraying the role and services of the HRs. But the dichotomy in accounting between human and non-human capital is fundamental ; while the later is recognised as asset and placed in the financial statement, the former is not considered by the conventional accountants.[17] According to Taylor and Glautier, "accounting information originates essentially from the results of financial transactions .... the only transaction which is recognisable (in case of HR) is the contractual obligation to make a periodic payment in return for periodic services under the wage agreement. Hence wages and salaries are treated as current costs in the manner as rent payments for land leased by the firm, for neither is owned as assets."[18] The rationale of such a statement is that something can be considered as asset only when the entity can claim legal ownership in one hand and the entity should posses it with the expectation of deriving services from it in future. As the HRs, associated with organization, fail to satisfy these two criteria they, therefore, cannot be treated as asset.

The incipient analysis regarding the inclusion of HRs within the purview of accounting system was considered during early sixties. In 1964, Hermanson suggested an 'unpurchased goodwill method' for valuation of human assets.[19] However, his work did not make such impact on the contemporary accountants in favour of incorporating HRs in financial statements. In 1967, in the Harvard Business Review, Hekimian and Jones emphasised that information on HRs should be used in the planning process and also in the resource allocation decisions.[20] In the same year Rensis Likert, in his writing, pronounced the importance of human assets accounting and the relative consequences of accounting for HRs in the organizations.[21]

In the years of 1968 and 1969, R. Lee Brummet and others[22] described the various proposals on HRA in different journals.

The "Human Resources Accounting system" is found to be applied first in the annual report of R.G. Barry Corporation during 1969 (R.G. Barry Corporation, Annual Reports, 1969-73). Some notable institutions in America, Japan and Europe were inspired with the idea of presenting data on HRs. The list includes American Telephone and Telegraph, General Motors, AB Valvo of Sweden, Mobile Oil, Proctor and Gamble, General Telephone and Electronics and others.[23]

The Committee of American Accounting Association (AAA)[24] and the American Institute of Certified Public Accountants (AICPA) also opined in favour of HRA. They remarked that this concept will influence the people of both public and private organizations.

Moreover, some authors also take up the cudgels for the measurement and valuation of HRs. Notable among them are M. Scott Myers and V.S. Flowers (California Management Review, Summer, 1974), Richard B. Frantzrel, Linda L.T., Landau & Donald, P. Lindberg

(Business Horizon, 1974), Bikki, Jaggi and Hon-Shiang Lau (The accounting Review, 1974), and Wayne J. Morse (Accounting and Business Research, Winter 1975). In eighties and early nineties also authors across the world are pondering over the issues and are finding means and ways of applying the models to the real world situations.

V

Human Resource Valuation Models

Now discussion on some of the major HRA models developed so far is in order.

A. **Historical Cost Method :** This model was first developed by Rensis Likert and his associates [25] at R.G. Barry Corporation in Ohio Columbia (USA) in 1967. According to them, the expenses incurred on recruitment, training and familiarization, experience building should be capitalised in one group. In another group, information on the investment made for supervisory or managerial personnel or group of individuals for routine or current services may be obtained from basic documents, such as invoices, current vouchers etc. The total value so incurred are to be allocated over the accounting periods the employees expected to remain within the organization. In other words, the total value is being amortized annually over the expected length of services of individual employees. The unexpired cost is considered to be the investment in HRs. The technique of HRA under this method is partially similar to the method of accounting of other inanimate resources. The model is also designated as the cost-based HRA technique. The model is based on the following assumptions :

(i) Capitalisation processes are to be adopted for the recording of investments in HRs.

(ii) A suitable amortization process is to be followed for recording of such capitalised amount.

(iii) Losses due to obsolescence of investment in certain skill or knowledge capabilities are to be identified and recorded.

(iv) The dynamic nature of investment on HRs is to be reported.

How the different types of historical cost based expenses are grouped, capitalised and amortized is shown diagramatically by Brummet[23]. See diagram below.

TABLE - 1
A Generalized Model of Cost-Based Human Resource Accounting System

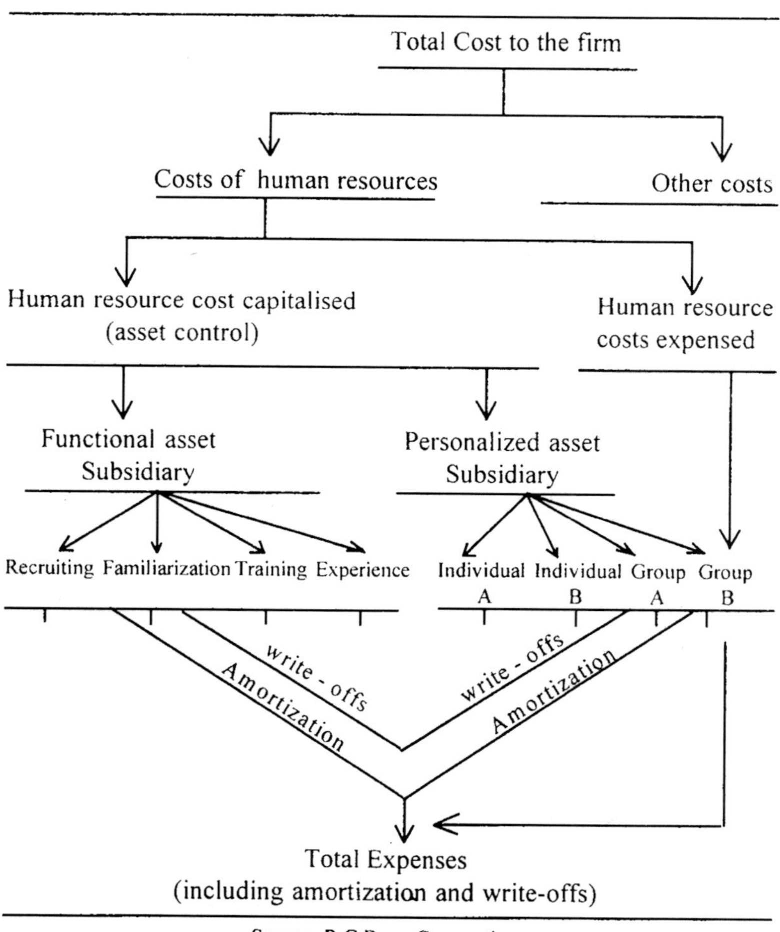

Source : R.G.Barry Corporation

This method of analysis helps control and maintain subsidiary accounts of investments balances by function, by individuals, department or project teams.

Accounting Treatments

Expenses incurred on the recruitment, training, experience building of various personnel in the organization and capitalisation of their values can be accounted for through the following journal enteries.[27]

1. Investment in Human Resources A/c ....Dr.

   To Profit & Loss A/c
   (Being the expenses incurred on recruitment, training experience building, advancement of HR capitalised).

2. Profit & loss A/c ....Dr.

   To Deferred Income Tax A/c.
   To Retained Earnings A/c.
   (Being the 50% of Income on capitalisation transferred to deferred Income Tax A/c. and 50% to Retained Earnings)

When the capitalised cost is amortized the reverse entries will be :

1. Profit & Loss A/c ....Dr.

   To Investment in Human Resources A/c.
   (Being the amortization of capital cost).

2. Retained Earnings A/c ....Dr.

   Deferred Income Tax A/c...............................Dr.
   To Profit & Loss A/c.

(Being the amortized portion recovered from Retained Earnings and deferred Income Tax provided earlier).

Criticism

1. The value of HRs computed under this model can hardly project the real value of the services potentials of HRs.

2. Such information is of little use for measuring the total value of the organization.

3. Since these costs are historical in nature and such assets cannot be disposed of, information on them are not of much significance for investment decisions.

B. **Replacement Cost Method :** In order to overcome the limitations of the historical cost method, Hekimian and Jones developed a method for valuing the HRs. According to them, the current cost of replacing the present set of workers by another set with similar efficiency and experience may be considered the value of HRs. Eric G. Flamholtz[28] opined that replacement cost may be necessary for two reasons : one relating to an individual and another to position.

(i) The first one relates to the cost incurred by the management for replacing one employee by a new employee with equivalent skill, ability and knowledge for better result. In other words, the costs incurred represent the individual's value to the firm.

(ii) The second one relates to the value of series of services expected to be derived from an employee at the respective positions he holds and will hold at present as well as in future. It implies that an individual generally moves in different positions during his total tenure of his service life. Hence the positional replacement cost refers to the current cost of replacing the series of services expected from an employee during his total stay at different positions in the firm.

The expected realisable value of an individual may be calculated by taking the following factors into consideration :

(a) 'Mutually exclusive' states or positions that an individual will occupy are to be defined.

(b) Value of each position is to be determined.

(c) The total tenure of services of an individual is to be estimated.

(d) The probability that an individual will hold the expected positions during his total stay with the organization.

(e) The Probability that an individual will not leave the organization is to be determined.

The expected realisable value[29] E (RV) of an individual to an enterprise will be determined with the following formula :

$$E(RV) = \sum_{t=1}^{n} \left[\sum_{i=1}^{m} \frac{R_i - P(R_i)}{(1+r)^t} \right]$$

Where, R_i = Value R (i.e. benefit) that can be derived by the organization in each possible service state 'i'.

P(Ri) = Probability that a person will hold the position 'i'.

m = Position at the time of exit (after holding each position)*,

n = Number of years an employee is expected to stay with the firm,

r = Appropriate discount rate,

t = Time.

The model with some variation has been operationalized at Lester Witte 7 company, CPAS in Chicago and is reported as a case study in some detail in the book by Caplan and Landekich[30].

Criticism : The model is criticized on the following grounds:

1. The measurement is based on probability estimates, which may not be accepted universally.

---

* It refers to cost involved, as a person holds various positions throughout his service career.

2. The Psychology behind replacement of present set of employees with another set is not considered here.

3. The calculation involved are debatable, critical and expensive.

4. The replacement of some employees, who are indispensable to the organization may not be possible.

Despite such limitations, this method pin points that the contributions from different positions that an individuals holds during his stay with an enterprise should be considered while valuing its HRs.

C. **Opportunity Cost/Competitive Bidding Method**

For overcoming the difficulties associated with the measurement of HRs as per the replacement cost method, the concept of opportunity cost was proposed by Hekimian and Jones.[31] The opportunity cost of HR is the Value of an individual employee in alternative uses. According to the authors, the opportunity cost is the best means to value an individuals. The value may also be established by competitive bidding within the organization. A human asset, therefore, will have a value only when it is a scarce resource, i.e. when its employment in one division denies it to another division, the amount payable by the division or department with the highest bid will be opportunity cost of that particular HR.[32] The model can bė justified on the ground that an optimum benefits can be derived from an employee because he is placed in the various positions only through competitive bidding process.

Criticism : The arguments against these views are as follows :

1. Here valuation of HRs are based on bidding process. It cannot be accepted as logical as employees are not placed in different positions adhering to such principles.

2. The scope of hiring of personnel of similar efficiency, experience and skill are not considered here.

3. Since all the alternative uses of an individual's service available in an organization are not identifiable, application of the method is not feasible.

4. Valuation of performance of an individual in terms of profit is not practicable.

The method is eye-opener in the sense that an employee should be engaged in such a way that the company can be benefitted to its optimum level.

D. **Capitalisation of Salary Method :** This model was propounded by Baruch Lev and Aba Schwartz.[33] According to the authors the valuations of HRs of homogeneous group can be done by aggregating the present values of the wages and salaries payable to individual employees during their stay with the organization. Each individual has an earning ability for the services he rendered to the firm. This earning profile is represented by his productivity which is again depended on his age. As he becomes aged, his productivity may diminish due to the technological obsolescences, deterioration of health etc. Thus all these factors lead to the reduction in annual earnings.

Measurement of HR under this method involves the following considerations :

1. Divisions of employees according to their age, grade of pay and designation.

2. Determination of the average annual earnings per employee in each group.

3. Calculation of the total earnings based on the remaining tenure of their service life.

4. The total earnings will be discounted on the basis of average rate of return on investment.

The human resources can be valued on the basis of the following formula :

$$V_{\lambda} = \sum_{t=\lambda}^{T} \frac{1(t)}{(1+r)^{t-\lambda}}$$

Where, V_λ = The human capital value of a person 'λ' years old,
T = The person's retirement age,
$I(t)$ = The person's annual earnings upto retirement,
r = A discount rate specific to the person.

This model was refined later by the authors considering the possibility of death of an employee before his retirement. Then the formula stands as below :

$$E(V_y^*) = Py \sum_{t=y}^{T} (t+1) \sum_{i=y}^{T} \frac{I_i^*}{(1+r)^{t-y}}$$

Where, $E(V_y^*)$ = Expected value of the human capital value of a person 'y' years old.
T = Person's retirement age.
$Py(t)$ = Probability that a person dying at age 't'.
I_i^* = Expected earnings of the person in period 'i'
r = Discount rate specified to the person.

Criticism : This model is criticized on the following considerations :

1. An individual may leave an organization prior to his retirement, death or due to various factors whether personal or impersonal. Those factors are not considered here.

2. The promotional aspect of an employee is not highlighted here. It may appear as if there will be no personal betterment of an individual during his service life.

3. The ratios based on the value of HRs calculated through the application of this model is of little consequences to the investors and management.

4. The discounted factor may vary from firm to firm, as there is no specific rate for such valuation.

5. The cost of recruitment, selection, training, placement and retaining the HRs are not considered here.

6. Here the underlying assumption is that the benefit derivable from an employee just equal to the cost of salary paid to him. If that be the case, there is no need of valuing HRs.

Despite the above limitations, it may be claimed that the application of this method of valuation is least debatable, as data on the basis of which such values will be determined are objective in nature.

E. **Economic Valuation Model**

The theme under this model resembles to that under the capitalisation of wages and salaries model. The only difference is that under the Economic Valuation Model[34], the aggregate of the services expected to be derived from employees are capitalised whereas under capitalisation of wages and salaries method the earnings profile of employees are capitalised. The value of an individual to an organization may be defined as the present value of the future services of employees expected to be derived during the total period of his association with the organization. The present worth of services of an individual is determined by multiplying the expected future services by the rate of pay. The product arrived at is discounted by the rate of return on investment. Here an individual during his total period of service life is expected to occupy various positions and performs different activities during this period. The question generally arises as to the probability of the changes is position of an employee and the scope of deriving services from him. Moreover, the probabilities of individual's leaving the organization before his retirement or death are also considered here.

The total expected service of an individual in an organization may thus be obtained as follows :

$$E(S) = \sum_{i=1}^{n} Si \; P(Si)$$

Where, E(S) = The expected total service value.

Si = The service expected to be derived from each state to be occupied by the employee.

P(Si) = The estimated probability of the expected service being actually derived.

This model is being regarded as the most rational in comparison to other models as it makes provisions for an ex-ante economic value of human resources.

Criticism

1. Since the economic values of individuals are measured here separately, values created by them jointly as a group are not considered here at all.

2. An objective measurement of the probability of stay of an individual with the organizations at different positions, his services rendered to the organization, other employees' eagerness to stay with the organization etc. is very difficult.

3. It is very fastidious to measure separately the value of the services or individuals.

F. **Return on Efforts Employed Method :** Under this method value of HRs are not measured directly, here, individuals are evaluated in order of efforts they exert for the benefit of an entity. In other words, unlike other methods where the valuation of HRs are based on salaried paid to them or services derivable from them, here performances of the individuals are measured in terms of the efforts they give to earn the profit of an enterprise. In this method, efforts are measured on the basis of three factors, viz. the positions he holds, the degree of excellence he achieves and the nature of his experience. Contributions of individuals as well as contributions of a group are measured in terms of efforts rendered. The method may be explained with the following illustration :

(a) An entity has four levels of performances, Viz.

(i) directors,
(ii) managers,
(iii) foremen, and
(iv) workmen.

(b) The efficiency of its employees may be classified in three groups, viz.

(i) excellent,
(ii) good,
(iii) satisfactory, and

(c) The experience of an employee may be classified into four categories, viz.,

(i) upto 2 years,
(ii) upto 5 years,
(iii) upto 10 years and
(iv) above 10 years.

Values may be assigned to each of the above variables according to their intensity.

(a) **Levels and grades of work**

Nos.	*Job Grade*	*Factors i.e. Weight*
10	Directors (Production)	10
8	Managers (Production)	8
6	Foremen	6
3	Workmen	3

(b) **Efficiency of Individual Performance**

Personal Assessment	*Factors*
Excellent	2.0
Good	1.0
Satisfactory	0.5

(e) Experience and efficiency which increases on ascending order

Years of Experience	*Factors*
0-2 years	1.2
2-5 years	2.5
5-10 years	5.0
Over 10 years	7.0

Now, weights or factors of three characteristics of an individual should be multiplied to determine the efforts employed in each individual For example, efforts employed by a foreman with 5 years experience and good performance are to be measured as (6x1.0x2.5) = 15. The sum of the products thus obtained from all employees in production department represents the total efforts employed by the department. Now when the total profit of an organization is determined then the profit earned should be expressed per unit of efforts. For example, if the total profit earned is Rs. 4,00,000 and the total efforts employed in the entity is 2,000, then the average rate of return on human efforts will be (Rs. 4,00,000 ÷ Rs 2,000) = Rs. 200. The method helps interdepartmental, inter-area and inter-firm comparison and also assists the management for efficient planning and control of the business.

Some consider that, this method has some similarities with the R O I method of efficiency measurement technique used in financial accounting. This information also helps management in making efficient HR allocation among the departments and divisions. According to Glautier and Underdown, if there is any variations in the performances of human efforts year to year, the question may arise as to cause of such differences. Hence how the difference can be overcome should be sorted out[35].

Criticism

1. Where the objective of HRA is to value the HR asset of an organization, this system is unable to provide any plausible way in measuring the value of the same. On the other, it only provides an index of efficiency of HRs of an organization.

2. The numerical factors assigned to each variable are not verifiable. Moreover, the ratings awarded to the different levels and grade may not be appropriate according to the respective contributions. As such this unscientific rating may create dissatisfaction among the efficient employees.

3. Although the efforts exerted by an individual is an important information to the management and also to others but it is difficult to measure here the efforts in monetary terms to get the economic value of an individual in the organization.

4. The ratings awarded to different individual may vary from organization. As such this measure does not help in inter-firm comparison of HR performances.

G. **Value Measurement Method :** H.R. Hermanson[36] suggests that value of an employee to an entity should not be based on the discounted value of his earning alone. The relative efficiency of the entity in the economy should also be reckoned with in this context on the ground that because of the efficiencies of all the individuals in the entity, the organization has achieved an edge in the economy. The author proposes the following steps to be taken into consideration for valuing HRs of an entity.

(i) Determination of wage payment to different levels of management for succeeding five (5) years.

(ii) The wage payment is discounted at the rate of return earned on assets of the firm for the most recent year.

(iii) The discounted value is being multiplied by the firm's efficiency ratio yielding an approximation of the present value of future services of the firm's human resources.

The "efficiency ratio " of an individual is determined by :

$$\text{Efficiency Ratio} : \frac{\text{Firms' Rate of return (based on 5 year's average)}}{\text{Average rate of return (for 5 years) of all firms in the economy}}$$

Criticism

1. In this uncertain world it is very difficult to forecast future cash flows and to ascertain objective discount rate.

2. Since forecasting of incremental earning and expenditure is subjective in nature, HR values measured on this basis is debatable.

3. Even an inefficient employee under this method will be valued at higher rate, because his earnings also will be multiplied by the firm's efficiency ratio.

These limitations notwithstanding, it is the method which alone attempts to measure the human resources on the basis of the relative weights the market gives on an entity.

H. **Non-Monetary Measurement :** Previous measurement models are based on the values of rewards or benefits the organization can obtain from the employees. In other words, they are based on monetary benefits derived from ultimate outcomes expressed in monetary terms. But outcomes are the results of some contributing actors which are not usually expressed in monetary terms. In other words, the earlier method does not established a casual relationship between the human organization, its output and the variable signifying to measure that output. Likert and Bowers[37] devised a system with an object of showing a casual relationship. They considered non-monetary measures such as work rate, attitude measures, employee turnover etc. most important in their model and accordingly incorporated the items in their models.

According to them the determinants of a group value is based on - (i) Casual Variables, (ii) intervening variables and (iii) end-result variables. The casual variables are independent and can be manipulated by the management. They refer to managerial behaviour which reflects the strategy, skill, leadership and policy-making ability of management. These factors again influence the intervening variables like organisational estimates, peer leadership, group process and subordinates' satisfaction. These variables again lead to the end-result variables of productivity, cost of production, sales and profit etc. With the help of information on these items attempt can be made to measure the magnitude of correlation between the variables. It will point out the overall human efficiency.

The relationship among these variables may be reproduced as below :

TABLE - 2

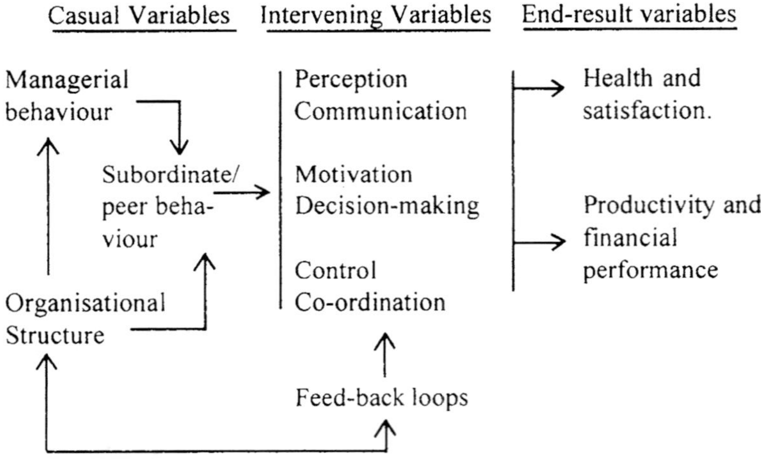

Human Resource Accounting - An Empirical Relational System
Source : Likert and Bowers (ref. 19 p. 7)

The HR valuation, under this method, will be measured by predicting the firm's future earnings which is depended on the causal and intervening variable. These will be discounted to get the net present value of the business and a proportion of this value may be allocated to HR value.

Criticism

1. The practicability of the method is open to question because it is very difficult to establish a causal relationship between various behavioural variables and performance variables as suggested in the model.

2. The method attempts to measure HR values as a group. It does not try to evaluate separately the end-results contributed by individuals. Hence application of this model does not help identify by inefficient employees.

Despite such limitations, if the end-result variables like output quality, manpower turnover rates, profits etc. are carefully reported along with causal and intervening variables, atleast the changes in the end-results can be explained by changes in the causal or intervening variables. It may help in introducing corrective steps.

An alternative process of measurement is suggested by Flamholtz identifying the individual's value based on social, psychological and economic determinants. According to him the individual's value to an organization can be measured in terms of the present worth of potential services he could render during the total period of his service life in the organization, and secondly, on the probability that the individual will remain with the organization[38].

An Appraisal

In the previous section major models on HR valuation have been discussed in brief. In some aspects they are similar and in some points they differ. Let us examine them for selecting one of them which can be most suitably applied for accounting in NPOs.

In the *Historical Cost Method* the underlying assumption is that the present value of the series of services expected to be derived from the employed during their stay with the entity equals the amount spent for their selection, training etc. In other words, through spending money on human resource development, the organization is expected to be benefitted with their present and future services. But it is very difficult, if not impossible, to measure the duration, volume or magnitude and values of such services as nothing has been clearly defined on these respects. The discount factor, essential for the capitalisation of service values, is not considered in this model. The initial expenditure incurred on training, placement and development of personnel are taken into consideration perhaps on the assumption that the personnel will stay with the organization till retirement. Even though the model provides an objective measure of the HRs, it cannot serve our purpose for its unability to supply an indication as to the services expected to be derived from them in future.

The *Replacement Cost Method* has also its limitations. The basic feature of the method is that it attempts to incorporate the impact of advancement in production methods arising from the rapid change in technology and economic situations. To cope up with the advancement, the present set of HRs require to be replaced by a new combination. The cost of replacement is not highlighted here. Though it provides a major improvement over the historical cost method, it cannot be applied in practice because of the lack of objective information on the replacement cost of employing the present army of employees.

The *Opportunity Cost Method* also neither consider the value and volume of services, nor make a provision to consider the discount factor. Moreover, if it is applied, the employees may raise the following questions : Which type of opportunity of them is considered here ? What are the alternative uses they have ? Who are bidders in the organization? Theoretically, the model does not provide any answer to these questions. Two departments in an organisation usually do not compete with each other for receiving services of an individual employee. It may be possible in those organization which is less specialised and where workers of each department are capable of performing duties equally well in different organizations. In modern times, multifarious activities are required to be performed for smooth functioning of an organization. That apart, specialised training is imparted to employees to make them suitable for a particular department according to its peculiar need. They are not developed with object of making them competent for bidding. Hence, the application of the model does not appear to be feasible.

The *Capitalisation of Salary Method*, which is popularly known as Lev and Schwartz model, is considered logical and practicable as it takes into account emoluments paid to the employees, their stay with the entity, the discount factor while capitalising their earnings to have a measure of the human resource value. It is assumed here that, the volume of services expected to be derived from the date of appointment to the date of retirement follows a fixed pattern. This appears to be static to some extent. Despite such shortcoming this system can provide an objective assessment, though to some extent, of HR value. That is why, the organization reporting HRA, generally value their HR on the basis of this model.

Under the *Economic Valuation Method* values of the services provided by the individual during his service life rather than the salaries they receive, are capitalised for the purpose. The method is logically sound for it considers the benefit derived from the labour of the employees. The benefit derivable from such labour may not always equal to the sacrifices made to acquire the service. Sometimes benefits may be higher, sometimes they may be lower than the emoluments paid to the employees. Unlike Lev and Schwartz model, here marginal rate of return of wages are not considered equal to the marginal rate of return of money. In other aspects, however, the two systems are similar. But the problem with the system is that it is very difficult to have an objective and separate measure of the value of services of individual employees. Because of this difficulty of quantifying such benefits it is very difficult, if not impossible, to apply the method for measuring HRs of an enterprise.

The basic assumption under the *Return on Efforts Employed Method* is that the whole of the return earned by an organisations is contributed by the employees alone. But this argument is not tenable. The return is the result of various factors of production. In order to make the organization operative and successful the managements' participation can be overlooked. A major part of the profit is the outcome of the pricing policy formulated and implemented by the management. People at the lower and the middle level are directed by the top level management to achieve the desired object. Therefore, the managements' contribution should be duly reckoned with. That apart, the business as a whole is valued first through capitalising the total return earned by the entity. Then the cost of other assets are deducted from such capitalised value to have a measure of HR value. This round-about way of measurement is arbitrary in nature. This residual value may be contributed by the goodwill or other factors. Moreover, the method is dependant on the discounting factor and the volume of profit. Any variation in the estimate of the former may lead to a heavy fluctuation in the measure of HR values. Thus, this method fails to provide separately the value of individuals to the entity. However, through measuring the points assigned to an individual a rough estimate may be computed. But that is fraught with so many subjective items that the information they provide appears to be less dependable. Because of these difficulties this method is not usually used for measuring HR values.

Application of the *Value Measurement* techniques for gauging the HR values is very arduous. The underlying assumption of deriving services from the employees for forthcoming five years is contentious. Moreover, the system of multiplying the capitalized value of the earning of the employee by the efficiency ratio does not stand on sound footing for employee performances are over emphasised through double counting. It may be the fact that due to the higher rate of payment to the employees their productivity is enhanced. If we capitalise the higher rate of payment first and again we multiply it by entity's relative efficiency, then the efficiency is counted twice. Hence the valuation is inflated. The model has some resemblance with the Lev - Schwartz model as to the method of capitalisation of salaries. Here, capitalised value of salaries of all employees are multiplied with firm's efficiency ratio. It may be interpreted that all the employees are equally efficient. But it cannot be the case. If the management wants to measure the value of individual employee they will be misguided. Because there will be every possibility that an inefficient employee may be overvalued at the cost of another efficient employee. Anyway, the peculiarity of the model is that it attempts to consider the relative efficiency of the entity in the economy. This point is important, no doubt, but if we want to make it logical we should first be sure that rate of return from the spending on salary is at par with the other assets of the entity. But that is a formidable task. Hence the application of the model is not practicable.

In the case of *Non-Monetary Measurement Method*, the technique of qualifying HR values is very complex and confusing. Here, the end-result may somehow be measurable, but it is very difficult to quantify the causal and the intervening variables. The process of conforming the non-monetary variables to monetary variables, all the non-monetary items are to be quantified first and at the end the amount of service derivable from an employee is to be measured. For such a measure, the managerial leadership, organizational climate are to be quantified, which will help us in gauging the intervening variables of peer leadership, group process etc. so that end result variables like productivity of employees and the financial performance can be correctly measured. Questions may generally arise whether it is, at all, feasible to quantity these variables. Therefore, we can quantify these variables, we cannot subsequently capitalise them to get the HR value. Although a positive correlation among the three variables has been concluded by several authorities, the application of this method is not practicable for lack of objective and dependable data.

On the basis of the above discussions on the various concepts, it may be inferred that even though most of the above models appear logically sound in appropriate cases, it is not possible to apply most of them in practice because of lack of suitable and proper data, and inability to have objective measurements of all the variables mentioned in the models.

But the application of Lev-Schwartz model, where the value of services derived from the employees are capitalised is operationally feasible. That is why, the present study has attempted to value the HRs of a NPO based on this model. Details of the model are given in Chapter six which is engrossed in measuring the value of HRs to a NPO.

VI

HRA Practices in India

Let us have a glimpse of the HRA practices adopted by different organisations in India. Here, the HRA is yet to be used as a universal system of accounting. Moreover, the Indian Companies Act, 1956 does not make it compulsory for a company, whether it is a public one or private one to report on HRA in their financial reports. A few organizations, however, of their own value their HRs and report them annually as a supplement to their accounting reports. A list of those companies in India, are given below :

(a) Public Sector Organisation :

1. Bharat Heavy Electricals Ltd. (BHEL).
2. Cement Corporation of India (CCI).
3. Engineers India Ltd. (EIL).
4. Electrical India Ltd. (EIL).

5. Hindustan Shipyard Ltd. (HSL).
6. Oil India Ltd. (OIL)
7. Oil and Natural Gas Commission (ONGC).
8. Project and Equipment Corporation of India (PECI).
9. Minerals and Metal Trading Corporation of India (MMTC).
10. Steel Authority of India Ltd. (SAIL).

(b) Private Sector Organizations :

1. Tata Engineering and Locomotive Works (TELCO).
2. The Associated Cement Company (ACC).
3. Southern Petro-Chemical Industries Corporation (SPIC).

HRA reporting practices of steel Authority of India Ltd., a Public sector undertaking, is given here as an example.

Steel Authority of India Limited.

Social Balance Sheet

Liabilities	*Rs. (in crores)*	*Assets*	*Rs. (in crores)*
Organisation equity	456.89	Social Capital Investments :	
Social equity	17940.89	Land	9.92
		Residential & other Buildings	332.90
		Roads & Bridges	26.93
		Water Supply & Sewerage	40.09
		Furniture & Fittings	3.16
		Other Equipments	43.89
		Human Resources	17940.89
	18397.78		18397.78

VII

TABLE - 3

HRA System in India Practised by the Different Companies

Sl. No.	*Name of the Company*	*Published HRA information since*	*Model adopted*	*Discount Factor Considered*
1.	Bharat Heavy Electricals Limited (BHEL)	1974-75	Lev and Schwartz	12%
2.	Cement Corporation of India Limited (OCI)	1980-81	Lev and Schwartz with refienments as suggested by Flamhotz and Jaggi & Lau.	15%
3.	Engineers India Limited (EIL)	1980-81	Not reported	10%
4.	Oil and Natural Gas Commision (ONGC)	1981-82	Not reported	12.25%
5.	Minerals and Metal Trading Corporation of India Limited (MMTC)	1983-84	Lev and Schwartz	12%
6.	Steel Authority of India Limited (SAIL)	1983-84	Lev and Schwartz with refienments as suggested by Flamhotz and Jaggi & Lau.	14%
7.	Metallurgical and Engineering Consultants (India) Limited (MECON)	1984-85	Lev and Schwartz	14%
8.	Madras Refineries Limited (MRL)	1985-86	Lev and Schwartz	15%
9.	Oil India Limited (OIL)	1984-85	Lev and Schwartz	10.5%
10.	National Thermal Power Corporation Limited (NTPC)	1986-87	Lev and Schwartz	12%
11.	Associated Cement Companies Limited (ACC)	1983-84	Lev and Schwartz	Not reported
12.	Southern Petro-Chemicals Industries Corporation (SPIC)	1983-84	Lev and Schwartz	Not reported

The information as provided in Table '3' (see p. 39) reveals that most of the enterprises in India, reporting HRA in their annual accounts, adopted the Lev-Schwartz model for valuation of their HRs. BHEL, one of the leading undertakings in India, is the pioneer in implementing the concept, publish HRA since 1974-75 based on the Lev-Schwartz model. However, SAIL, another frontline undertaking in India adopts the Lev-Schwartz model with modifications suggested by Jaggi, Flamhotz and Lau.

One point is to be noted here that in most cases the discounted factor is around 14%. But the rates ranges from 10% to 15%. The logic of considering such values of this factor is not mentioned in the report. However, the maximum of the rates (i.e. 15%) is near to the rate of interest on fixed deposit payable by a nationalised bank in India during the period of study.. The maximum rate is used for discounting with a view to providing a conservative measure of the HR values.

VIII

Requirement for Introducing HRA in Non-Profit Organizations

So far in India HRA has been practised very little, and whatever small has been done in this direction that has been confined to profit-seeking organizations only. The basic reason for such limited spread of the idea is perhaps that the conventional accounting system is capable of reflecting, though to a less extent, how far the basic objective of earning profit has been realised. Non-adoption of HRA therefore, does not make any barrier to reflect the profit earning capacity of the business.

But in welfare organization, HRA is needed because, in most of the cases the objective of an entity is to render services rather than to earn proit. Such services flow from the people associated with the organization. The users of accounting information, the public in general and the funding agencies in particular, are interested in learning the prospect of the flow of services and the sources of the flow of such services. HRA of welfare organization, it is discussed earlier can serve such purpose.

The need for HR information in the financial reporting of NPOs arises from the following three bits of information :

(a) How much services does the NPO contribute to society ?

(b) How much are sacrificed by the people of the NPO for rendering such services ?

(c) What is the value of the stock of these services ? That means, what are the values of the people associated to the NPO ?

As the existing accounting system of NPOs is unable to highlight the information on the above aspects, some additional information should be provided along with the traditional accounting reports by these organizations. For the purpose we are to study first the existing system of financial reporting of NPOs, their limitations and how such limitations can be overcome. These issues are discussed in the following chapters.

References

1. American Accounting Association, "Report of the Committee on Human Resource Accounting", *The Accounting Review*, Vol. 48, Supplement, 1973, P-169.

2. Sidney Davidson, Clyde P. Stickney, James S. Schindler and Roman L. Weil, *Accounting : The Language of Business*, 2nd edition, Thomas Horton and Daughters, Glen Ridge , N.J. 1975, P-25.

3. Eric G. Flamholtz, *Human Resource Accounting*, Dickenson Publishing Co. Encino, California, 1974, P-3.

4. R. Lee Brummet, Eric G. Flamholtz and William C. Pyle (eds), HRA : *Development and Implementation in Industry* (Michigan : Braun and Brumfield, Inc 1969) P-111.

5. G. C. Sinha, "Accounting for Human Resource" *Accounting Theory*, Book World, Calcutta, First edition, 1989 (PP 258-76).

6. Eric G. Flamholtz, "*Human Resource Accounting*", Dickenson Publishing Co., Encino, California, 1974, pp 11-16.

7. R.K. Gupta, *Human Resource Accounting, Managerial Implication*, "Value of and Accounting for Human Resource ", Anmol Publication 1988, Ch. 3, pp 40-45.

8. Rensis Likert, *The Human Organization : Its Measurement and Values*, McGraw-Hill, New York, 1967, pp 84-95.

9. Roger H. Hermanson, "Accounting for Human Assets", Michigan State University, Graduate School of Business Administration, Bureau of *Business and Economic Research*, Occasional Paper No. 14, East Lansing, Michigan, 1964, pp 4-5.

10. American Accounting Association, "Report of the Committee of Human Resource Accounting", *The Accounting Review*, Supplement to Volume XLVIII (1973), P-169.

11. M.W.E. Glautier & B. Underdown, *Accounting Theory and Practice*. "Accounting for Human Resources", Pitman 1983, P-164.

12. Eric Flamholtz, "Towards a Theory of Human Resource Value in Formal Organization. "*The Accounting Review*", Jan. 1971, pp 667-668.

13. P.K. Ghosh, Maheswari and Goyale, *Studies in Accounting Theory*, "Human Resource Accounting", Wiley Eastern Limited, New Delhi, 1990. p-490.

14. Baruch Lev and Aba Schwartz, "On the use of the Economic Concept of Human Capital in Financial Statements : A Comment". *The Accounting Review*, Jan. 1971, pp. 103-112.

15. R.K. Gupta, "Value of and Accounting for, Human Resources", *Human Resource Accounting, Managerial Implication*, Anmol Publication, New Delhi, 1988, pp. 48.

16. Alfred Marshall, *Principles of Economics*, Macmillan, London, 8th Edition, 1964, P-409.

17. M.W.E. Glautier and B. Underdown, op. cit., P-164.

18. P.J. Taylor and M.W.E. Glautier, "Accounting Information and Industrial Relations : Social Implications and Cost and Benefit Considerations", *Economic Research Papers*, University College of North Wales, Bangor, 1974, pp. 7-8.

19. Roger H. Hermanson, "Accounting for Human Assets", Michigan State University, Graduate School of Business Administration, *Bureau of Business and Economic Research*, Occasional Paper No. 14. East Lansing, Michigan 1964, p. 6.

20. J.J. Hekimian and C.H. Jones, "Put People on your Balance Sheet", *Harvard Business Review*, Vol. 45, No. 1, Jan-Feb. 1967.

21. Rensis Likert, "The Human Organisation : Its Management and Value McGraw Hill Book Co. New York, 1967, p. 1.

22. R. Lee Brummet, William C. Pyle and Eric G. Flamholtz, "Accounting for HR", *Michigan Business Review*, March, 1968.

- R. Lee Brummet, Eric G. Flamholtz and William C. Pyle, "HR Management--A Challenge for Accountants", *The Accounting Review*, 1968, pp. 217-30.

- R. Lee Brummet, Eric G. Flamholtz and William C. Pyle "HRA : A Tool to Increase Managerial Effectiveness" *Management Accounting*, August, 1969.

- R. Lee Brummet, William C. Pyle and Eric. G. Flamholtz : "Human Resource Accounting in Industry", *Personal Administration*, July-Aug. 1969.

- R. Lee Brummet, Eric. G. Flamholtz and William C. Pyle (eds) "HRA - Development and Implementation in Industry", *Foundation for Research in Human Behaviour*, Ann Arbor, Michigan, 1969.

23. R. Lee Brummet, *Handbook of Modern Accounting* (edited by Sidney Davidson & Roman L. Weil), "Human Resource Accounting", Mcgraw Hill Book Co., Second Edition, Ch. 37, N.J. 1975, pp. 1-29.

24. - American Accounting Association (AA), "Report of Committee on HRA", *The Accounting Review*, Supplement to Vol. XLVIII, 1973. pp 169-185.

- American Accounting Association (AAA), "Report of the Committee on Accounting for Human Resources", *The Accounting Review*, Supplement to Vol. XLIX, 1974, pp. 115-124.

25. Based on the research work by W.C. Pyle with the R.G. Barry Corporation, "Human Resource Accounting". *Financial Analyst Journal*, Sept.-Oct. 1970, pp. 69-78.

26. R. Lee Brummet, "Human Resource Accounting", *Handbook of Modern Accounting* (edited by Sidney Davidson & Roman L. Weil), McGraw Hill Book Co., Second Edition, Ch. 37, N.J. 1975, pp. 1-79.

27. G.C. Sinha, op cit, pp. 264-265.

28. Eric G. Flamholtz, "The Theory and Measurement of an Individual's value to an organization", Ph.D. Dissertation, University of Michigan 1969, and A Model for Human Resource Valuation : A Stochastic Process with Service Rewards", *The Accounting Review*, April 1971, pp. 253-267.

29. Eric G. Flamholtz, "HRA, Measuring Positional Replacement Cost", *Human Resource Management*, Vol. 12, No. 1 (Spring 1973), pp. 8-16.

30. Edwin H. Caplan and Stephen Landekich, "Human Resource Accounting -- Past, Present and Future", *National Association of Accountants*, New York, 1974, pp. 68-69.

31. J.J. Hekimian and C.H. Jones, "Put People in your Balance Sheet", *Harvard Business Review*, Graduate School of Business Administration, Harvard College, Harvard, USA, Jan-Feb. 1967, Vol. 45d, No. : 1.

32. M.W.E. Glautier and B. Underdown, *Accounting Theory and Practice*, "Accounting for Human Resources", Pitman, 1983, p. 168.

33. Baruch Lev Aba Schwartz, "On the use of the Economic Concept of Human Capital in Financial Statement", *The Accounting Review*, Jan. 1971, pp. 103-112.

34. R. Lee Brummet, Eric G. Flamholtz and William C. Pyle. "Human Resource Management - A Challenge for Accountants". *The Accounting Review*, April, 1968.

35. M.W.E. Glautier and B. Underdown. "Accounting for Human Resources", *Accounting Theory and Practice*, Pitman, London, 1976, pp. 724-726.

36. Roger H. Hermanson, "Accounting for Human Assets", Michigan State University, Graduate School of Business Administration, *Bureau of Business and Economic Research*, Occasional Paper No. 14, East Lansing, Mich 1964, pp. 7-11.

37. Rensis Likert, The Human Organization : Its Management and Value, McGraw-Hill Book Company, New York, 1967 : "Human Organizational Measurements : Key to Financial Success, "*Michigan Business Review*, May 1971 ; with William C. Pyle, "A Human Organization Measurement Approach, "Financial Analysts Journal". January-February, 1971.

38. E.G. Flamholtz, "Assessing the validity of a Theory of Human Resource Value : An exploratory Field Experiment / Study", University of Columbia, 1973.

3

Nonprofit Organizations and their Various Aspects

Introduction

Application of the sophisticated models discussed in the previous chapter requires a study of the present accounting principles practised by the NPOs. But because of the absence of specific laws, regulations etc. (which are mandatory in nature) uniform accounting principles and practices in the area have not crystallised. Under the circumstances, the major principles as presented in various literatures are briefly discussed in the present chapter. From this study we are to find out the principles and practices that are most common in use. Then only an attempt can be made to enquire how the value of HRs, associated to NPOs, when measured according to HRA model selected in the previous chapter, can be accommodated in the existing accounting system of the NPOs.

With this end in view, this chapter discusses first the meaning of a NPO, or in other words, why these organizations are termed as such ? Section two delineates the various features of such entities, while section three describes how such features influence the accounting principles of NPOs. The purposes this accounting information serve is highlighted in the fourth section of the chapter. While the major differences between the profit seeking organizations and non-profit organizations are analysed in section Five, the basic accounting prinçiples practised by the NPOs for reporting is presented in section Six. Finally, in the form of appraisal the last section draws attention to the short-comings of the existing reporting of the NPOs in satisfying the objectives for which the organizations are formed.

I

Meaning of NPO

At this stage of civilization organizations can be divided in two broad groups ; the profit organizations (POs) and NPOs. The ultimate goal of POs is the 'earning of profit', but in case of NPOs, the primary intention is to serve the community interest rather than to individual self-interest.[1] Hence, 'pro-bono publico' work or voluntary public service is the prima facie objective of the welfare NPOs. In other words, the POs are generally go for the profit, but the primary objective of NPOs is to provide services to the society as a whole irrespective of caste, creed and religion. Lousiana Non-profit Corporation Act, 1948 defines, non-profit organization means an organization organized for a purpose not involving pecuniary profit or gain to its shareholders, or members, provided that the organization may pay reasonable compensation and salaries for services rendered.[2] Lloyd Morey and Glen G. Yankee Opine, non-profit involves a break-even concept of operation.[3] The basic idea is that entities are organized to render service to some segment of population at the cost of performing the service without financial gain to the persons or groups who supplied the funds used in furnishing the services[4]. A NPO is, therefore, an economic entity that provides, without profit, a service beneficial to society and that has an equity interest which cannot be sold or traded.[5] It is noticeable in the preceeding defination that the term 'without profit' is generally the sole motive of the NPOs, but it is not intended to imply that an organization may not plan for and, in turn, attain some excess of income over expenditure during a particular period of time of its operation.[6] This 'surplus', so created can be applied for greater volume of services performed by the organization without accruing any benefit to the equity of the NPOs. Therefore, the existence of NPOs becomes inevitable as they provide services to those who could not, by virtue of the purchasing power available to them, acquire the socially desirable amount of services provided by the POs.

However, NPOs range from large and complex to the small and simple ones. They include hospitals, colleges and universities, religious organizations, associations, foundations, cultural institutions and the voluntary social service organizations. The voluntary welfare organizations are selected for out study, since in this area wholehearted involvement of HRs is indispensable for achieving the objective of such organizations. Hence, in the present study, the term NPO will be considered to mean welfare organizations, though the former is a more comprehensive term.

II

Features of NPOs

The ultimate goal of a PO is to earn profit primarily for its owners, while the fundamental objective of a NPO is to serve the some members of the society, usually other than those contributing fund to the organization. The generation and distribution of services rather than earning of profit is the primary objective of NPOs. Here the objective of rendering services are far more important than that of acquiring and controlling wealth. Hence, the basic feature of NPOs are as follows :

(i) The organization has no profit responsibility[7] - the sole motive being to serve the people of the society freely or at below cost.

(ii) They are meant for providing services to various sections of the society.

(iii) These organizations are mostly run with the resources from funding agencies, who neither expect return of their donations nor desire benefit in kind, proportionate to the resources they provide.[8]

(iv) The organizations gain distinctions on the basis of their contribution to the society, rather than on the customers and owners' satisfaction.

(v) Here neither individual nor joint ownership can be conceived of. Since the entity on behalf of the society is considered the owner, its ownership neither be transferred nor be sold[9] to individuals.

(vi) Generally control of these organizations is bestowed to the persons having interest in rendering particular type of service. These entities are thus controlled by people who have no recoverable investment in them.[10]

(viii) The financial information provided by these organizations are meant for enabling the present and potential contributors and donors to decide whether they continue their support and assistance in favour of the organization in future as before.[11]

III

Impact of the Features of NPOs on Their Accounting System

Accounting is considered to be the information system which collects financial data and converts those data into information for communicating them to the users both within and outside the organization (e.g. organizers, resource providers, general public etc.).[12] It is applicable to NPOs too.

The accounting system of an organization is designed by its objectives, whether it is a profit seeking or a non-profit seeking organization. Keeping in mind the features of the two kinds of entities and the particular environments in which they operate, one can realise the accounting methods practised by these organizations. An organization, without an aim to earn profit, is not required to report in its profitability. On the contrary, the management of the POs are very much aware of their responsibility of reporting the owners the net income earned during the period concerned and the extent to which such resources are used in achieving them. For NPOs such information is not required as the fund providers are not interested in it.

Based on the features of NPOs, discussed earlier, it may be inferred that most of these entities adopt a system of accounting which is arranged for recording the inflow and outflow of their financial resources. This is why developed the system of preparing Receipts and Payments Accounts. Since the survival of these organizations is based on the donations and contributions of funding agencies, and in some cases funds are earmarked for specific uses, the principle of "Fund Accounting"[13] is practised by most of the NPOs for financial reporting.

Since these organizations do not bear profit responsibility, here the accounting system is not geared to report the same. On the contrary, Statement of Revenues and Expenses has been designed to reflect the surplus or deficit of revenue over expenses incurred during a period, so that the organizers can gauge how far their means can meet resource requirements to achieve their objectives.

The most important features of the NPOs is that these entities are set up with a view to providing services to the people of the society. The financial reporting should provide information according to that. But the conventional accounting system followed by these entities, it appears, does not make provision for measuring and reporting the intensity of the services rendered by the organization during an accounting period.

Because of the absence of the ownership claim in a NPO, its accounting system is not required to make provision for drawing up capital accounts. Similarly, there is no scope for opening Profit and Loss Appropriation Account which is meant for showing how much accrues to the owners at year end.

As the services are usually rendered freely or at token prices, cost of such services are not generally ascertained. Accordingly, the problem of recovering cost of services provided to the beneficiaries does not arise. This is why the concept of maintenance of capital usually are not applied here. In most of the cases depreciation accounting are not practised. The issue is discussed later in greater length.

Unlike POs, here the issue of valuing fixed and current assets does not draw much attention, for continuity of a NPO depends on the magnitude of services provided to the society rather than on the value of the assets it holds.

Keeping in mind these influences of the features of NPOs on their accounting, let us examine in the next section the accounting principles and practices adopted in such organizations.

IV

Objectives of Accounting and Financial Reporting in NPOs

On the light of the features of the NPOs discussed above, it is evident, the generation of services and distribution of the same voluntarily to the weaker section of the people are the primary objective of these organizations. But resources are life-blood of all organizations, since they provide services. The present and potential resource providers are interested in the organization's performance and in the information on how its managers have discharged their stewardship responsibilities. Hence, the financial reporting of these organizations should provide information which is useful in assessing stewardship and performance.[14]

The fundamental tenet of a society is based on the belief that these NPOs are entrusted with public resources and they are restricted by the funding authorities to utilise those resources for specific purpose. Violations of these mandates may impinge upon an organization's financial performance or on its ability to continue to provide a satisfactory level of services[15] and also have an adverse affect on assessing the performance of management in discharging their stewardship responsibility. Again, the concept of stewardship accounting requires that such a system should have the following characteristics.[16]

(i) It should always concern with safeguarding the assets.

(ii) It should always be cautious about the efficient utilisation and management of the assets.

The objectives of financial reporting by non business organization have been outlined in the Statements of Financial Accounting Concepts (SFAC), published by the Financial Accounting Standard Board (FASB). They can be summarised below :

(i) Financial reporting should provide information about the performance of a NPO during a particular period so that the present and potential resource providers may take rational decision on their future contribution to the organization.

(ii) Such reporting should furnish information on the efficiency of the personnel engaged in the organization in discharging their stewardship responsibility to the funding agencies.[17]

(iii) The report should supply information on the utilisation of scarce resources[18] and allocation of the same in the most efficient manner possible for the benefit of the people of the society.

(iv) Such statement should give information on the service efforts and accomplishment of an organization.

(v) It should indicate the change in the amount and nature of the net resources of a NPO.

(vi) Such reporting should furnish indication as to the liquidity (Cash and other liquid assets) position of the organization.

(vii) Such report should be such that it would make the information more informative by representing the performance of the associated people on the services rendered by them to the society.

(viii) Financial reporting should provide information on the effects of events that have already happened. No future amounts or events are involved here.[19]

(ix) Such reports should provide information to the present and potential users about the services provided by the non-business organizations, its efficiency and effectiveness in providing such services and its ability to provide those services.[20]

(x) Accounting reporting of NPOs should be such that it provides information to the other users like the creditors in assessing the prospects of receiving their dues.[21]

(xi) These reports should also furnish information on the cash flow potential of the organization[22].

(xii) Financial reporting should be such that through the information the funding agencies can make up their mind regarding where to contribute and how much to contribute.

(xiii) Accountability to public is essential, since the public support these organizations through direct contributions and grants. Many special privileges, such as tax-exempt status may be enjoyed by the resource providers on such contributions.[23]

Although, the traditional accounting system of NPO, through the application of stewardship accounting, aims to provide some information to the resource providers but the basic objective of reporting[24] information on achievement of organization's goal remains unuttered. This issue is highlighted later in this chapter.

V

Objectives and Accounting System of POs - A Comparison

Before proceeding further let us compare first between the two types of organizations in respect of their environment, objectives and accounting system etc.

Environment : The environments in which POs and NPOs are similar[25] in many ways. They generally perform their operations with the resources available to them to satisfy the human wants. Our social environment also restricts the improper utilisation of the natural and physical resources.

Therefore, the limited resources are utilised in the most efficient manner by the organizations to attain their respective objectives. The two types of organizations are alike in this respect and both are responsible to the resource providers as well as to the society to justify their commitment. Both incur obligations, are bound by the government laws and regulations and are subject to incur and pay taxes.[26] In some ways or other, the same donors provide funds to these organizations. Both the organizations are accountable to those who provides resources or to their authorised representatives.

Difference between the POs and NPOs arises due to the difference in the objectives of the organizations. The major dissimilarities between these two entities can be summed up as follows :

Objective : The POs operate with the sole objective of providing benefits to those who contribute resources to them, but in case of NPOs, the major objective is to provide services usually to the weaker section of the society.

Ownership : The contributors, in case of POs generally claim the ownership of the organization in which they contribute capital. But in case of NPOs, no individual ownership can be claimed since there is no individual equity interest. Here control is generally vested in persons having an interest in the particular service provided by the organization[27]. Thus the NPOs are usually organized and managed by people other than the contributors who have no recoverable interest in the organization.

Length of Business : The NPOs generally wind up either when the contributions from various sources are inadequate for performing usual operations or where the desired goal, for which the organization is set up, has been achieved and which need not be pursued further. But in case of POs it is upto the discretion of the owners to decide on the existance and perpetuity of the entity.

Basis of Accounting : The basis of accounting of the NPOs is different from that of POs because of their incongruity in attitude and span of existence. Where the POs, because of their greater span of life, follow the accrual basis, the NPOs, on the other, generally welcome the cash basis of accounting.

Focus of Accounting : The NPOs generally follow the accounting principle based on the 'stewardship accounting'[28] concept, where funding agencies impose restrictions as to the use of the vested resources. In case of POs, the management also acts as steward, but such restrictions are not imposed and the executives here are at liberty to use the resources to earn profit for the benefit of the owners.

Accounting for Capital Expenditure : For POs long-term expenses are capitalised and are shown as assets in the Balance Sheet. Depreciation on such assets are charged to the Profit and Loss Account. But most of the NPOs usually do not capitalise such expenses. The reason for capitalizing the fixed assets are that benefits from the assets expected to be derived from such expenses will continue for more than one year and the cost should be recovered from the customers proportionately year after year by way of depreciation. But in case of NPOs, the recovery of such expenses usually does not play such an important role. That is why, the cost of fixed assets are usually written off as and when they occur. ·

Sources of Funds : The various sources of funds of POs include profits from operation, sale of fixed assets and investments, issue of shares and debentures, raising of loans etc. In case of NPOs, the inflow of resources comprises of contributions from donors, grants from state and central governments and other bodies. Anyway, NPOs usually do not have internal source of financing like retained earnings of POs, because these organizations are meant for rendering services rather than for earning profit.

Treatment of Surplus/Profit : Difference between income received by way of subscriptions, collection from beneficiaries etc. and expenses incurred for providing services, in case of NPOs, is termed as 'surplus' or 'deficit'. This 'surplus' or 'deficit' is transferred to capital fund or general fund which represents the value of resources at the disposal of the organization to be used for the benefit of the people of the society. In case of POs this 'surplus' or 'deficit' is termed as 'net profit' or 'net loss' which is transferred to capital account as it accrues to owners.

Performance Measurement : The measuring rod of the performance of the POs is the net profit earned by them during an accounting period. The higher the profit, the better the performance of the organization. But the performance of the NPOs is evaluated by the extent of services rendered by them. The traditional accounting system of NPOs, however, does not highlight this aspect[29]. The efficiency of POs is measured by the ratio of return on investment (ROI) which is calculated through dividing the value of services by the value of resources utilised for the purpose. This issue has been discussed in detail in chapter Four.

Control Through Budgets and Standard Costing : The POs use standard costing and budgetary control techniques to ensure efficient planning and control of the organization. Budgets are used to project the future and standard costing is used to evaluate the performances at floor levels. For NPOs there is usually little scope for introducing standard costing. Budgets play a vital role in such cases. Spending mandates given by resource providers, generally take one or two forms : a) specific budgetary appropriation or, b) restriction imposed by donors. For instance, a budgetary appropriation may limit the amount that a welfare organization can spend for flood relief. Thus, budgets in POs work as an instrument for planning, whereas in case of NPOs, they work as a control device in the hands of resource providers[30].

VI

Accounting Principles and Practices of NPOs

The accounting practices followed by most of the NPOs are described here briefly. Efforts are made to reflect in the financial reports the contributions received from the donors and grantors and the expenditures incurred by the organizations in providing services to the society. But practices vary from organizations to organizations as to the basis of accounts, system of earmarking resources donated by the granting authorities, accounting for fixed assets, the method of allocating such costs over the life of the assets, the system of presenting annually the difference between income and expenses and the financial statement of affairs at the year end. This section makes an attempt to jot down the accounting principles and practices adopted by the NPOs on the above issues.

1. **Basis of Accounting :** On what basis should the events be recorded in accounts of NPOs ? Should the events be recognized as and when they occur ? Or should they be recorded when case is received or paid for them ? Or should the recording begin on the basis of mixture of the two system ? The defination of the National Council of Government Accounting on the basis of accounting is noteworthy in the context. There the basis of accounting is defined as "when revenues, expenditures, expenses and transfers — and the related assets and liabilities — are recognized in the accounts and reported in the financial statements"[31]. There are three methods used to determine when various amounts are transacted and placed in the accounting records. They are :

(i) Cash basis

(ii) Accrual basis, and

(iii) Modified acrual basis.

Cash Basis of accounting is a system where only the cash transactions are taken into consideration. Many nonprofit organizations still adopt the cash basis of accounting because they often do not want to recognize income prior to the actual receipt of cash.[32] This practice is justified when receipt of donations and subscriptions are not ensured. In accrual basis, it is the accrual of income and expenses related not only to the current period but also to the preceeding and succeeding period are accounted for. Under this method the financial position of the organization can be portrayed on a more realistic basis[33], since one of the principles of accounting i.e. the matching principle[34] is adopted here for reporting the various revenues and related expenses of such entities in their financial reporting. Of the two, accrual accounting generally provides a better indications of an organization's performance than does information about cash receipts and payments[35] because it recognizes that the acquisition of resources needed to provide services and the rendering of services by an organization during a period often do not coincide with cash receipts and payments of the period[36].

The modified accrual basis of accounting is considered by some NPOs. In this method of accounting, incomes are recognized when they are received in cash but amounts payable are recorded as liabilities on accrual basis[37]. This method is most conservative on the sense that it makes provision for liabilities, but does not recognize a promise for subscription or donation as gain until it is realised in cash.

The NPOs, generally the voluntary charitable units, publish their reports on the accrual basis of accounting perhaps on the expectation as to the certainty as to getting donations and grants from funding agencies on the basis of which organizations can spend money for the benevolent activities.

2. **Fund Accounting :** This method of accounting is practised to accommodate the peculiar nature of NPOs. Donors may earmark resources for specific uses. Hence the fund should be segregated. The concept of fund accounting is based on the principle of segregating resources into a number of self-balancing sets of accounts on the basis of restrictions imposed by the contributors and governing body[38].

The term 'fund' here has been defined as "a sum of money or other resources segregated for the purpose of carrying on specific activities or attaining certain objectives in accordance with specific regulations, restrictions or limitations and constituting and independent fiscal and accounting entity".[39] (National Committee of Government Accounting, 1951, P. 234).

Generally, most of the NPOs follow the concept of fund accounting because of the opinion that this method of accounting is the most appropriate method of exercising the stewardship control over funds. Although a number of such organizations are not in favour of this recommendation on the belief that this leads to make the financial reporting too confusing. Earlier various funds were treated as completely separate accounting entities and were represented separately in the balance sheets for separate funds. Now, in recent days most of the non-profit entities follow the method of eliminating the several funds and combining them in a restricted number.

According to Emerson O. Henke, the principal object of 'fund accounting' is fiscal control.[40] That means, the revenues from each funds and utilisation of the same during the fiscal period are shown simultaneously in the fund account so that how much of the resources donated for a particular purpose can be known as and when necessary.

NPOs usually segregate the funds under some broad headings, namely :

(i) Unrestricted operating fund
(ii) Restricted operating fund,
(iii) Fixed assets fund,
(iv) Endowment fund,
(v) Expendable and non-expendable fund,
(vi) Working Capital fund,
(vii) Capital project fund.

They are discussed here in brief.

Unrestricted Operating Fund : This fund represents those resources which may be expended to carry out the primary purposes of the organization and are not stipulated for any specific object. This implies that the income under this fund can be used in any manner, any time to achieve the desired objective of the organization. This fund is based on the principle of accrual basis of accounting.

Current Restricted Operation Fund : This fund is also referred to 'specific purpose fund'. Here the resources available to the organization can be expended for specific operating purposes only.

Fixed Assets Fund : This fund represents the fixed assets owned by the organization. This fund is restricted by the authority to be used only for the additions to fixed assets. Depreciation may be provided on such assets and in that case the depreciation on the asset is also charged to this fund account.

Endowment Fund : The principal of this fund is kept preserved. The interest accrued from this fund can be utilised either for restricted or for general purpose. After the expiry of the specific time the principal of the fund is utilised by the governing board in accordance with the gift agreement. There may be different types of endowment available to the organization. They are :

(i) **Simple Endowment :** Here gifts received from external parties can be utilised in perpetuity, keeping the principal intact.

(ii) **Term Endowment :** Here gifts are contributed by individuals specifying the respective dates or events after which the fund can be expended.

(iii) **Quasi Endowment :** Here such fund is created by the governing board itself. This fund is formed out of unrestricted gift received and accumulated in the unrestricted current fund.

Expendable and non-expendable Fund : Expendable funds are those where the entire resources may be expended for current operations. But in case of non-expendable funds the principal must be maintained in tact. Where the expendable funds are comprised of revenues, grant, gift and bequests the non-expendable funds include capital fund and various endowment funds.

Revenue Fund : This fund is created primarily out of short term income. It can be categorised into general fund and specific or special purpose fund. The general fund for taxes and other revenues are restricted for specific uses.

Working Capital Fund : This fund is formed out of the gifts, bequests from contributors or transfer from other funds. The funds may be utilised for purchases of assets or for repayment of loans.

Capital Project Fund : This funds are created through the issue of special bonds and receipt of grants from government and gifts from various sources for specific capital project. A separate fund is created for each of such capital projects.

3. **Accounting for Fixed Assets :** As fixed assets play a vital role in the functioning of an organization, accounting for fixed assets perform a leading part in accounting literature. The services rendered by the NPOs are mostly derived from the performances of the human resources associated with the organization. Although the HRs are indispensable, their performance depends on the inanimate assets of the organizations. In absence of these resources, people engaged with the entities will not be able to perform their work efficiency. Such assets are acquired either through direct donations or through purchase when sufficient funds for the same are available.

Accounting for fixed assets is necessary basically for two reasons : One, for representing in the balance sheet the value of the resources at the disposal of an organization and two, the recovery from the sales price of the consumed portion of the assets by way of charging depreciation. The voluntary welfare organizations consider that these resources are not so important in NPOs since current valuation of fixed assets is of little consequences here. Among these organizations only a few of them account for capital expenditure. According to these NPOs, the fixed assets of these entities cannot be termed as security for the payment of debt obligations and therefore, may not be defined as the basis of credit and hence, cannot be recorded in the balance sheet. Organizers of some other NPOs, also opine in the same line on the ground that there is need of matching income with expenses and that such a situation helps pleading poverty as a means of raising funds.[41]

Application of generally accepted practices about accounting for fixed assets is difficult in NPOs. Generally, three alternatives are used here for accounting for fixed assets.[42] They are :

(a) Immediate write off,
(b) Capitalisation of fixed assets, and
(c) First write off and then capitalise.

Immediate write off : The expenses made on purchase of fixed assets is treated as expenses and shown in the statement of income and expenditure by the NPOs. The logic of writing off of the assets is perhaps that the cost of the same need not be recovered from the beneficiaries of the services. Hence, the question of recovering the capital consumed through uses does not arise here. The concept, however is not at par with the generally accepted accounting principles followed in profit seeking organizations.

Capitalisation of Fixed Assets : This method is the most widely accepted and used method of accounting for fixed assets. According to this method, the assets purchased are shown in the Balance Sheet.

The logic behind the approach is that, fixed assets are major assets of the entities and for that the board is accountable to the competent authority and failure to reflect these assets in the balance sheet is considered misleading.[43] The major disadvantage of capitalisation is that it renders the financial statement more complex. An unsophisticated statement reader may conclude that an organization has more funds available for current spending than it actually has.[44]

This method, however, conforms with the generally accepted accounting principles adhered to in profit seeking organizations.

Write Off and then Capitalise : As per this method, the assets acquired at the expenses made on purchase of these assets are written off immediately by showing the amount as expenses in the income and expenditure account and then the expense is capitalised by showing the amount in the balance sheet as fixed assets on one hand and capital or general fund on the other. However, this method is said to be inconsistent with accounting convention,[45] and is not in accord with the generally accepted accounting principle (GAAP).

4. **Accounting for Depreciation :** Such an accounting is the corollary to the accounting for fixed assets. In fact, depreciation is the distribution

of the cost of an assets over its estimated life. It is charged on the assets to reflect the fair value of the asset on the financial position statement. It is provided to determine the cost of resources consumed in performing certain work or carrying out an operation. Moreover, to assess the net income earned by a profit seeking organization, depreciation is treated as an item of expense. Generally the POs calculate depreciation on the various assets owned by them and charge it to the profit and loss account, while they show the depreciated value of the assets in the balance sheet. However, in NPOs, where profit earning is not a concern, the depreciation is not charged to the income and expenditure account. That apart, there is no obligation to amortize or write off the cost of the investment over its estimated life. Again since there is no immediate outflow of cash for depreciation, no provision need be made in the budget.[46] For the same however, the GAAP are in favour of charging depreciation on the fixed assets in NPOs.[47] The depreciation accounting in such organizations is preferred on the following reasons :

(i) It helps in measuring the actual cost of services rendered or goods purchases.

(ii) The net revenue earned during a particular period cannot reflect the true picture unless the depreciation is taken into account. On the contrary, if the cost of fixed assets is written off in the year of acquisition, the outflow of cash for expenses for the year will be highly exaggerated.[48]

(iii) Where the NPOs are under legal obligations to income tax to government, depreciation should be taken into consideration as an item of expenses to reduce tax liability.

(iv) The NPOs generally operate on grants and donations from various sources. If depreciation is shown as an item of expenses, the financial position will appear comparatively less sound and the excess of revenues over expenses will decrease. In such cases it will be easier to convince the granting agencies the need for greater amount of grants and donations.[49]

The system of accounting for depreciation in NPOs, when applied, should be similar to what is followed in the POs. If the cost of fixed assets are capitalised and the depreciation is not charged year after year in the income and expenditure accounts, the balance sheet will be overstated. Anyway, "assets used in providing services are both valuable and exhaustible. Thus a cost is associated with the use of exhaustible assets whether they are owned or rented, acquired by gift or by purchase or used by a business or a nonprofit organization."[50] Hence it is better to charge depreciation to the income and expenditure account of the NPOs.

5. **Financial Reporting :** The statement of position, issued by the AICPA Accounting Standard, does not recommend any specific format to be adopted by the NPOs for their financial reporting. On the other, it emphasises that the financial reporting should be such as to provide sufficient information appropriate for fair disclosure[51] and should be most suitable to the organization's need[52] in conformity with their objective. The basic financial reporting of a NPO should be represented through the following three statements :

(i) Balance Sheet,
(ii) Statement of activity,
(iii) Statement of changes in financial position.

The Balance Sheet of a NPO is designed to reflect the financial position of the organization by showing the assets, liabilities and the fund balances at the end of a particular period. A classified balance sheet may also be drawn to represent the 'current' and 'long term' assets and liabilities of the organization and the balance of 'restricted' and 'unrestricted' fund of the same entity.

Through the statement of activity the NPOs show the result of all the financial activities from the beginning to the end of an accounting period. This statement is also named differently such as, statement of support, revenue and expenses, capital additions and changes in fund balance or simply statement of changes in fund balance.[53] The Income and expenditure account, as practised by the NPOs in India and UK[54] is similar to this statement. Since these entities are not meant for earning profit, they maintain this account to determine the surplus or deficit of receipts over expenses during an accounting period as these entities can survive only when they have support of revenue and other additions equal to or it excess of expenses.[55]

The statement of changes in financial position provides the interested person with information about all the changes in financial position, including a summary of available resources and their use during the period.[56] The statement also highlights information on the methods of financing programmes on activities, investment of resources including capital additions, and changes in deferred support and revenue during that period.[57] The NPOs in India provides such information through the receipts and payments accounts (similar to Cash Book in British Method), showing the receipts as debit entries and all payments as credit entries in the statement. Finally the closing balance represents Cash and Bank Balance at the year end.

Presentation of Financial Statements

Even though a particular format for operating statement is not suggested, a simple but informative format for incorporating such particulars may be drawn as per Table-4, 5 & 6 for a voluntary welfare organization engaged in providing medical services to the society.

(See tables from p. 64 to 69)

TABLE-4
Wauwatosa Community Service Organization
Balance Sheet
June 30, 19X1

ASSETS			
Current assets :			
Cash	...	$ 79,000	
Pledges receivable	...	16,000	
Accounts receivable	...	48,000	
Inventory	...	25,000	
Total Current Assets			$ 1,68,000
Endowment fund Investments, at market			3,20,000
Building and equipment, less depreciation of $ 1,51,000			2,11,000
Total assets			$ 6,99,000
Liabilities and Fund Balances			
Current Liabilities :			
Accounts payable	...		$ 24,000
Current portion of mortage	...		7,000
Deferred gifts and dues :			
Membership fees	...	$ 18,000	
Plant fund gifts	...	25,000	
Restricted gifts	...	18,000	
Unrestricted gifts	...	3,000	64,000
Total current liabilities			95,000
Mortgage, 8% due 1989	...		75,000
Total liabilities			1,70,000
Fund Balances :			
Unrestricted, available for current operations	...	80,000	
Invested in Fixed assets, net	...	1,29,000	
Endowment fund	...	3,20,000	
Total fund balances			5,29,000
Total liabilities and fund balances			$ 6,99,000

Balance Sheet, Source : Gross and Washauer (Financial and Accounting Guide for Nonprofit Organizations, P-269), Ronald Press Publication, 1981

TABLE-5
Wauwatosa Community Service Organization
Statement of Revenue, Expenses, Capital Additions, and Changes in Fund Balances.
for the Year Ending June 30, 19X1

	Operating	Plant	Endowment	Total
Revenue & Support :				
Service fees	$ 1,55,000			$ 1,55,000
Grants, including $ 34,000 of restricted grants	61,000			61,000
Membership dues	53,000			53,000
Unrestricted contributions and bequests	35,000			35,000
Dividends and interest	16,000			16,000
Unrestricted realized and unrealized gains	18,000			18,000
Total revenue and support	3,38,000			3,38,000
Expenses :				
Program :				
Project A	1,05,000	$ 10,000		1,15,000
Project B	95,000	13,000		1,08,000
Membership services	40,000	4,000		44,000
Total Program	2,40,000	27,000		2,67,000
Supporting :				
General Management	38,000	2,000		40,000
Fund raising	6,000	1,000		7,000
Membership development	7,000	1,000		8,000
Total supporting	51,000	4,000		55,000
Total Expenses	2,91,000	31,000		3,22,000
Excess of Revenue and support over expenses	47,000	(31,000)		16,000
Nonexpendable Additions :				
Restricted gifts		20,000	$ 39,000	59,000
Restricted interest		1,000		1,000
Restricted realized and unrealized gains			17,000	17,000
Excess of revenue, support and nonexpendable additions over expenses	47,000	(10,000)	56,000	93,000
Fund Balances, Beginning of period	64,000	1,08,000	2,64,000	4,36,000
Transfers	(31,000)	31,000	-	-
Fund Balances end of period	$ 80,000	$ 1,29,000	$ 3,20,000	$ 5,29,000

Statement of activity. Source : Gross and Washauer (Financial And Accounting Guide for Nonprofit organizations, P-272). Ronald Press Publication 1981

TABLE-6
Wauwatosa Community Service Organization
Statement of Changes in Financial Position
for the Year Ending June 30, 19X1

Working Capital was Provided by :		
Current activities :		
Excess of revenue and support over expenses	$ 16,000	
Nonexpendable additions	77,000	
Excess of revenue, support, and non-expendable additions over expenses	93,000	
Add - Expenses not requiring outflow of working capital - depreciation	31,000	
Less - Income not providing working capital unrealized gains	(15,000)	$ 1,09,000
Net		
Proceeds of Mortgage	...	10,000
Sale of Investments	...	45,000
Deferred gifts and fees in excess of gifts and fees recognised as support	...	26,000
Total working capital provided	...	1,90,000
Working Capital was utilised for :		
Acquisition of fixed assets ...	(20,000)	
Acquisition of investments ...	(90,000)	
Repayment of bank loan ...	(7,000)	
Total Working Capital utilised ...		(1,17,000)
Net increase in working capital ...		$ 73,000
Components of change in working capital :		
Increase in current assets :		
Cash	$ 43,000	
Pledges receivable	2,000	
Accounts receivable	6,000	
Inventory	1,000	$ 52,000
Decrease (Increase) in current liabilities :		
Accounts payable	(5,000)	
Deferred gifts and dues	26,000	21,000
		$ 73,000

Statement of Changes in Financial Position. Source : Gross and Jablonsky (Principles of Accounting and Financial Reporting for Nonprofit organizations, P. 278), 1981.

The above statements are based on the American methods of presentation. Since the British system is adopted in India whether it is a profit seeking or a nonprofit seeking, for financial reporting, the above statements can be redrafted here accordingly (Table - 7,8 & 9).

TABLE-7
Wauwatosa Community Service Organization
Balance Sheet
as on June 30, 19X1

LIABILITIES	$	$	ASSETS	$	$
Fund Balances:					
			Building &		
Operating Fund :			Equipment	3,62,000	
Opening balance	64,000		- Depreciation	1,51,000	2,11,000
Add Excess of revenue, support and non expandable additions			Endowment Fund Investments		3,20,000
over expenses	47,000		**Current Assets :**		
	1,11,000				
Less Transfer to Plant Fund	31,000	80,000	Inventory	25,000	
Plant Fund :			Accounts		
Opening balance	1,08,000		receivable	48,000	
Add/(Less) excess of revenue support and nonexpendable additions over			Pledges receivables	16.000	
expenses	(10,000)		Cash	79,000	1,68,000
	98,000				
Add transfer from operating fund	31,000	1,29,000			
Endowment Fund					
Opening balance	2.64,000				
Add : excess of revenue, support and nonexpendable additions over expenses	56,000	3,20,000			
		5,29,000			
Mortgage 8%, Due :		75,000			
Current Liabilities					
Current portion of Mortgage					
Deferred Gifts and Dues :	7,000				
Membership dues 18,000					
Plant fund gift 25,000					
Restricted gift 18,000					
Unrestricted gift 3,000	64.000				
Accounts payable	24,000	95,000			
		6,99,000			6,99,000

TABLE-8
Wauwatosa Community Service Organization
Income & Expenditure Account
for the Year Ended on June 30.6.19X1

	Expenditures	$	$		Income	$	$
To	**Expenses:**			By	**Revenue & Support**		
	Project A	1,15,000			Service fees	1,55,000	
	Project B	1,08,000			Grants	61,000	
	Membership Services	44,000	2,67,000		Membership dues	53,000	
"	**Supporting Expenses**				Unrestricted - Contributions & bequests	35,000	
	General Management	40.000			Dividend & Interest	16,000	
	Fund Raising	7,000			Unrestricted realized & unrealized gains	18,000	3,38,000
	Membership development	8,000	55,000				
"	Excess of revenue and support over expenses		16.000				
			3,38,000				3,38,000

TABLE-9
Wauwatosa Community Service Organization
Statement of Changes in Financial Position
for the Year Ended on June 30.6.19X1

Sources of Funds	$	$	Applications of Funds	$	$
Excess of Revenue & support over Expenses	16,000		Working Capital Was utilized for :		
None-expendable Addition	77,000		- Acquisition of Fixed Assets	20,000	
	93,000		- Acquisition of Investments	90,000	
Add Expenses not requiring outflow of Working Capital Depreciation	31,000		- Repayment of Bank Loan	7,000	1,17,000
	1,24,000		Increase in current assets :		
Less Income not providing Working Capital - unrealized gains	15,000	109,000	- Cash	43,000	
			- Pledges receivables	2,000	
Proceeds of Mortgage		10,000	- Accounts receivables	6,000	
Sales of Investments		45,000	- Inventory	1,000	52,000
Deferred gifts and fees in excess of gifts and fees recognized as support		26,000	Decrease in Current Liabilities :		
Increase in Current Liabilities :			Deferred gifts and dues		26,000
Account payable		5,000			
		1,95,000			1,95,000

VII

An Appraisal

Unlike profit seeking organizations NPOs are created with the basic objectives of rendering services to the society. In case of profit seeking organizations the annual financial statements are capable of reporting how far the economic objective for which the firm is established has been achieved. In other words, earning profit, the chief objective of POs, is measured and reported in the annual financial reports. But in case of NPOs, the basic objective is rendering services usually at free of cost or below cost. Therefore, the basic objective of reporting should be presenting sufficient information about how far social welfare which is usually not in financial nature has been created. Accordingly, the traditional financial accounts of these entities are not meant for reporting how far the objectives for which the institutions are established. But it is a natural expectation that there should be an arrangement to report the extent of social welfare created in the period concerned. These points are already mentioned earlier. Now, let us examine how far the existing annual financial statements of NPOs capable of presenting these information.

The existing financial reporting system adopted by the NPOs, as discussed above, helps in providing information primarily on the sources from which the funds are collected, the volume of the individual sources, the restrictions on the use of them, the amount spent out of such resources, the earmarked funds, volume of unrestricted resources which are lying at the disposal of the discretion of the management. Information on the above are, no doubt, useful to the resource providers and others in making rational decisions.

The Activity account (vide page no. 80 of this thesis) does not, however, show the extent of activity of the previous year done by the organization. Rather it shows how much financial resources are collected and distributed for running the activity. It may be the case that the resources may be used, but welfare may not be generated at the desired level or the organization my provide social services at large extent with the use of meagre amount of resources. That means there may not be a cause and effect relation between the financial resources used and the welfare generated. The fees received or donations collected do not usually provide an indication as to the volume of social welfare created by the entity. That apart resources utilised may not reflect here the magnitude of sacrifices made by the people associated with the organization.

The basic objective of financial reporting of the NPOs as mentioned earlier (see page 50) is to report on the performances of the organization. But the information, for example, the fund balance, the value of current assets and current liabilities, the endowment fund investment, the various restricted and unrestricted fund balance etc. does not indicate or measure the performance in terms of organization's goal.

Evaluation of efficiency of an organization depends on the measurement of relation between input and output related to its activities. For profit seeking organizations the efficiency is measured in terms of return on investment (ROI). In NPOs the efficiency can be measured in terms of the rate of welfare generated against the efforts given by the various people namely, the employees, the organizers and the donors of the entity. Unless these two items are measured and reported it is very difficult to have an idea about the efficiency of a NPO. The activity account, the balance sheet and the statement of change in financial position make no provision to give an idea about the input in terms of sacrifices made by the NPO and the output in terms of the value of services rendered to different groups of people. Hence the objective of financial accounting of NPO on this account is not fulfilled.

Naturally the resource providers are interested in the effective use of their resources. That is why, various turnover ratios like debtors turnover, creditors turnover, stock turnover, fixed assets turnover etc. are used to test how efficiently the resources are utilised. Here resources used are measured and reported in terms of money because resources invested are converted in wealth which can be measured in terms of money. But in case of welfare organizations the resources involved are not money alone, but includes the whole-hearted efforts of the associated people. The traditional system of accounting of such organizations does not make any provision for reporting the same. So how effectively these resources are utilised is neither measured nor reported by these entities under this system of accounting. That is why the degree of efforts made by these NPOs and how far its target established earlier is accomplished cannot be gauged effectively. Thus the budgets or estimates prepared annually can reflect only on the estimates of annual monetary collections and expenses during the accounting period, but cannot provide information about the estimate of the expected services to be rendered during the concerned period.

The income statement (i.e. the Income and Expenditure Account) and the Balance Sheet are meant for reporting the result of economic events occurred during a particular period. This is why the income statement embraces purchases made or expenses incurred or assets acquired and revenues earned during the accounting period. Hence, the statement present in a nut shell the impact of all the annual economic activities of the entity. But in NPOs the conventional financial statements do not reflect the magnitude of activities performed during the period concerned. For instance, the financial statement of a charitable institution does not present how many patients are attended, how many of them are operated or how many people are relieved of their pains and pangs under the supervision of the entity. These organizations are basically meant for providing such services to the people of the society and accordingly that should be reported in their annual reporting. But the traditional accounting system as adopted by these organizations does not make a provision to report them. Hence, these statements cannot be claimed to provide correct reported on the events occured during the period concerned.

From the analysis it is evident that the existing system is capable of reporting the stewardship function of management, but it is very difficult to substantiate, the author thinks, the system provides information on the performance of the entity, the efficient use of the resources and other related matters. It is a fact that it is difficult to measure the performance of the organization (FASB, para 53), but unless a measurement of the same, however rough and ready that may be, is provided along with the statement it is very arduous on the part of the resource providers to evaluate the performance and efficiency of these entities. For the purpose two major bits of information is necessary :

(a) The value of the welfare created by the entity and the sacrifices made by the various people for the same, and

(b) The value of the sources of such services i.e. the value of the HRs involved in rendering such services.

The first one requires the measurement of the flow of services and the other one is related to the measurement of the stock of such services.

The next chapter i.e. chapter four attempts to derive a system to quantify and report such services through our accounting format and chapter six attempts to measure the value of such stock of services i.e. HRs. It is noteworthy in this context that this attempt does not aim to substitute the traditional system, rather it aims to supplement the same.

References

1. B. Barber, "Some Problems in the Sociology of the Profession," Daedalus (Fall 1963), pp. 669-688.

2. Haward L. Oleck, "Non-profit Corporations and Associations" - *Organization, Management and Dissolution*, Englewood Cliffs, N.J. 1958, Prentice Hall, Inc. p. 2.

3. This idea is subject to the criticism that prices to be collected from the beneficiaries for the services rendered to them need not be equal to the cost incurred for the services. However, the idea pinpoints that the price should not exceed the cost in such entities.

4. Lloyd Morey and Glen G. Yankee, "Accounting for Non-profit Enterprises," *Modern Accounting Theory*, edited by Morton and Becker, 1953, pp. 464-484.

5. Emerson O. Henke, "Accounting for Non-profit organizations," Wadsworth Publishing Company, Inc, Belmont Calif, 1966, p. 1.

6. Emerson O. Hanke, *Handbook of Modern Accounting*, "Found Accounting - Non-profit Organizations" edited by Sidney Davidson, Ch. 43, pp. 43.3 - 43.29. McGraw Hill Book Company, 1970.

7. Emerson O. Henke, Op. cit, p. 43.2.

8. Statement of Financial Accounting Concepts (SFAC) No. 4 : "Objectives of Financial Reporting by Nonbusiness Organizations", *Journal of Accountancy*, March 1981, p. 113.

9. Emerson O. Henke, Op. cit, p. 43.3.

10. Ibid, p. 43.3.

11. Statement of Financial Accounting Concepts, (SFAC) No. 4 : Op. cit, p. 113.

12. Herbert Leo, Larry N. Killough and Allan Walter Steiss, "Accounting and Control for Governmental and other Non-business Organizations," *Introduction to accounting and control for Governmental and other non-business Organizations*, Ch. 1, 1985, McGraw Hill Book Co., PP. 1.20.

13. Emerson O. Henke, Op. cit, p. 43.4.

14. Statement of Financial Accounting Concepts No. 4 - "Objectives of Financial Reporting by Non-business Organization", Journal of Accountancy, March 1981, p. 118, Para - 40.

15. Statement of Financial Accounting Concepts No. 4 - "Objectives of Financial Reporting by Non-business Organization", *Journal of Accountancy*, March, 1981, p. 115, para - 9.

16. M.W.E. Glautier & B. Underdown, *Accounting Theory and Practices*, "Objectives of Financial Reporting." A Pitman International Text 1976, p. 540.

17. SFAC Concept No. 4, *Journal of Accountancy*, Op.cit. para-40, p. 118.

18. Ibid, para 34, p. 117.

19. SFAC Concept No. 4, *Journal of Accountancy*, March, 1981, Op.cit. para-26, p. 116.

20. Ibid, para - 30, p. 117.

21. Ibid, para 31 & 46, pp. 117 & 118.

22. Ibid, para 45, p. 118.

23. Robert G. May, Gerhard G. Muller & Thomas H. Williams, "Accounting for public Sector Organization." *A brief Introduction to Managerial and Social uses of Accounting*, Prentice - Hall Publication, Inc. Englewood Cliffs, N. Jersey, 1975, pp. 59-84, Ch. 3.

24. Statement of Financial Accounting Concept No. 4 provides that the financial reporting of a NPO should be such that will help to assess the services provided by the organization to the society. Para-38, *Journal of Accountancy*, March, 1981, p. 118.

25. Statement of Financial Accounting Concept No. 4, Op.cit, para 14, p. 115.

26. Statement of Financial Accounting concept No. 4, Op.cit, para 14, p. 115.

27. Emerson O Henke, Op.cit, p. 43.3

28. M.W.E. Glautier and B. Underdown, Op.cit, p. 540.

29. SFAC Concept No. 4, *Journal of Accountancy*, Op. cit, para 53, p. 119 (The Traditional accounting system fails to measure the service accomplishments and research should be conducted to develop a system of measuring the service accomplishments.)

30. SFAC Concept No. 4, *Journal of Accountancy*, Op. cit. para 21, p. 116.

31. Herbert Leo, Larry N. Killough and Allan Walter Steiss, "Accounting and control for Governmental and other Non-business organizations". *Introduction to accounting and control for Governmental and other Non-business Organizations*, Ch. 1, McGraw Hill Book Co. pp. 1-20.

32. Emerson O. Henke, Op. cit., p. 43.19.

33. Statement of Financial Accounting Concepts No. 4 - Objectives of Financial Reporting by Non-business organization, *Journal of Accountancy*, March, 1981, Para 50, p. 119.

34. Robert W. Ingram, Russell J. Petersen, Susan Work Martin, *Accounting and Financial Reporting for Governmental and Non-profit Organizations : Basic Concept*, "Governmental Accounting Concept", McGraw Hill. Inc., 1991, Ch. 1, p. 9.

35. William Warshauer (Jr.), Malvern J. Gross (Jr.) and Joel W. Meyerson, - *Accountant's Handbook*, "Non-profit enterprises", A Ronald Press Publication, 1981, Vol. 2 6th edition, p. 43.5.

36. Ibid, p. 43.5.

37. Robert W. Ingram, Russell J. Petersen, Susan Work Martin, Op.cit, p. 37.

38. William Warshauer (Jr.) Op. cit. p. 43.5.

39. Emerson O. Henke, "Fund Accounting - Nonprofit Organization," *Handbook of Modern Accounting* edited by Sidney Davidson, 1970 Ch. 43, p. 43.4.

40. Emerson O. Henke, Op. cit, p. 43.4.

41. William Warshauer (Jr.), Op. cit, p. 43.7.

42. Ibid, p. 43.7

43. Herbert Leo, Op. cit., p. 439.

44. William Warshauer (Jr.), Op. cit, p. 43.7.

45. William Warshauer (Jr.), Op. cit, p. 43.8.

46. Emerson O. Henke Op. cit, p. 43.11.

47. William Warshauer (Jr.), Op. cit, p. 43.8.

48. Emerson O. Henke, "Accounting for Nonprofit organization - An Exploratory Study," *Bureau of Business Research*, Graduate School of Business, Indiana University, Bloomington, Ind., 1965.

49. William Warshauer, (Jr.), Op. cit. p. 43.29.

50. "Statement of Position - Accounting Principles and Reporting Practices for Certain Nonprofit Organizations", Issued by the AICPA accounting standards division in December, 1978, *Journal of Accountancy*, 1979, p. 98.

51. Herbert Leo, Op. cit., p. 3.

52. Statement of position, Op. cit. Para 36, p. 100.

53. Statement of position, *Journal of Accountancy*, Op.cit. para 25, p. 100.

54. William Pickles, *Accountancy*, "Receipts and Payments, and Income and Expenditure Account", The English Language Book Society and Sir Issac Pitman & Sons Ltd., London 3rd Edition 1960, p. 255.

55. Statement of position, Op. cit. para 30, p. 100.

56. Ibid, Para 33, p. 100.

57. Ibid, Para 34, p. 100.

4

An Accounting Model to Supplement the Existing Accounting System of Nonprofit Organizations

Introduction

The basic objective of financial reporting of a non-profit organization, we have already discussed, is to provide information useful for evaluating the effectiveness of the management of the resources in achieving the organization's goal.[1] Again, goal of a welfare organization is to provide services to the society. Hence, the effectiveness of the management of the resources requires measurement of the performances of the organization. Though it is difficult to measure such performances[2] we are to devise ways to provide information on the value of the services that the organization renders, the means with the help of which such services are generated (i.e. the sacrifices of the employees and the organizers) and the value of the stock of such services (i.e. the values of the people associated with the organization). It is evident from the previous chapter, the conventional accounting system of NPOs does not make provisions for reporting such information. This chapter aims to devise an accounting model to measure such services and report the same to the resource providers and other well-wishers of the organization.

With this end in view this chapter tries first to account for the flows of services rendered to the society and the resources and sacrifices necessary to generate such services. An accounting model is designed subsequently to incorporate the value of the services rendered by the employees and the organizer as well. Based on the model an attempt has been made to develop a system to evaluate the performance of the organization in achieving its objective. A series of related ratios have been projected to complete the appraisal. Having discussed the implications to these ratios to the people interested in the entity, the chapter suggests by way of conclusion that the model may be used to supplement the existing accounting system to make the information system mode useful.

I

Accounting for flows of sacrifices and services

Since the existing accounting system fails to provide the information on the quantum of services generated and distributed by the associated people, and the sacrifices made by them as well as the organization itself, a comprehensive accounting system of NPOs should, therefore, be so designed as to provide the following information.

(a) To indicate whether or not the entrusted funds are utilised according to the imposed restrictions.

(b) To report the volume of services rendered by the organization to the society.

(c) To disclose the sacrifices made by the selfless people of the welfare organization to generate such services.

(d) To impute in financial terms (even though it is very difficult to measure their values in material and objective manner) the value of these people to the organization.

(e) To gauge separately the contribution to the society made by the organization.[3]

Since the conventional system deals adequately with the first one, the proposed model humbly attempts to design an accounting model which may be capable of reporting on the other four.

NPOs, in general and voluntary welfare organizations in particular, are basically meant for rendering services to society with the financial assistance from the funding agencies and the sacrifices of the people associated with the organizations. The financial reporting of the NPOs, therefore, should thrash out two important properties, namely,

(a) Inflow of sacrifices from the beneficiaries in the shape of donations, sacrifices of the employees and the organizers, and

(b) Outflow of services to the beneficiaries and distribution of services involves the following steps :

(i) Receipts of sacrifices through :

(a) Collection of donations and subscription from interested parties and other various sources.

(b) employment of people who volunteer their services usually at free of cost or against a token salary.

(c) Sacrifices of the organizers.

(ii) Distribution of services through providing medical or other benefits usually at free of cost to the hapless people. In fact such services create social welfare, for activities of NPO make some individuals better-off and no one worse-off.[4]

The above particulars may be presented in the following proposed accounting model :

II

An Accounting Model (for Welfare Organization)

A 'Service and sacrifice account', similar to the Income and Expenditure Account adopted under the conventional accounting system, may be drawn up (vide page no. 81). The credit side of the account should show the value of the services rendered to the society (represented by SS) which is derived by deducting the collections (however small that may be) from the beneficiaries (Q), from the market value of services rendered to the society (P). The debit side of the account should present the contributions made by the funding agencies (D), the sacrifices of the employees (W_2) and the contributions of organizers (O). The contributions of the first group (i.e. D) and the token collection from the beneficiaries (Q) are used for paying goods and services acquired from outside (G), and for paying token salary to the employees (W_1). If from the excess of value of services rendered to the society over the collection from the beneficiaries (i.e. P-Q = SS), we deduct the contributions made by the donors (D) and the sacrifices made by the employees (W_2), we shall get measure of the contribution made by the organization (O) itself.

The net value of services rendered to the society (SS), therefore, depends on the contributions of the funding agencies (D), the sacrifices of the employees (W_2) and also the sacrifices made by the organizers (O). Relation among these variables may be symbolically presented as below :

SS = $f(D, W_2, O)$

Where, SS = Social surplus represented by the excess of the market value of the services rendered to the society over the token collection from the beneficiaries.[5]

Here, $D = G + W_1 - Q$

When, D = Contribution made by the donors.

G = Cost of goods and services procured from outside.

W_1 = Payments to employees as a token payment for their volunteered services.

G = Token collection from the beneficiaries.

Again, $W = W_1 + W_2$

When, W = Market value of the services rendered by the employees.

W_1 = Actual payment to employees made by NPOs as a token payment for their volunteered services.

W_2 = Sacrifices made by the employees, i.e. ($W - W_1$).

And, O = Contribution of the organization

$[\text{i.e. } O = SS - (D + W_2)]$

Finally, $SS = P - Q$

Where, P = Market value of services rendered to the society.

Q = Token collection from the beneficiaries.

When the relation among the variables are additive in nature, they may be put in the form of following equation,

$$SS \text{ (i.e. } P - Q) = [G + W_1 - Q) + W_2 + O$$

$$\text{or, } SS = D + W_2 + O.$$

The situation may be tabulated in the accounting model as under : (Table-10)

Table -10

Services and Sacrifices Account of ......
for the Year ending on ....

Sacrifices by benefactors			Services to beneficiaries		
1. Sacrificing of the funding agencies through :			4. Social services rendered		
			Market value of Social services	P	
Payment to Supplier of goods and Services	G		Less : Token collection from beneficiaries	Q	SS
Add Token Payment to dedicated employees	W_1				
	$G+W_1$				
Less Token collection from beneficiaries	Q	D			
2. Sacrifices made by the employees		W_2			
3. Sacrifice made by the organization (excluding employees)[6]	O				

The Rationale : The justification of such treatment may be described here in brief.

The beneficiaries of the services generated within a NPO, pay something, however small that may be. That is why, the value of net social services (SS) should be equal to the excess of the market value of services (P) over the token fees collected from the beneficiaries (Q). Since these items relate to the accomplishments or outflow in the hands of the organization they are shown on the credit side of the periodic account i.e. the service and sacrifice account.

The items relating to effort volunteered, i.e., the sacrifices necessary for achieving the accomplishments are shown on the debit side of the account. People rendering such services can be categorized broadly under these classes 1. Funding agencies, 2. Dedicated employees and 3. Organizers. The contributions of these three categories may be represented by D, W_2 and O respectively. Again the contributions from the funding agencies (D), alongwith the token collection from the beneficiaries (Q) are then utilised to meet the costs of goods and services procured from outside (G) and to make token payment to the dedicated people (W_1). the market value of services received from these people far overweigh the token payment made to them. The difference between the two amounts to their actual sacrifices and that is represented by (W_2). These people, however, would not avail themselves of the opportunity of making such sacrifices, had there not been such organizers. These organizations create a situation where the net value of the services rendered to the society exceeds the total of actual and imputed contribution of donors and employees (D + W_2). This surplus arising out of the sacrifices of all these three groups associated with an entity are placed on the debit side of the services and sacrifices account.

The above analytical information, although indispensable for representing the performance of NPOs, is not highlighted under the conventional accounting system. The income and expenditure account, as maintained under this system cannot portray fully the achievement of the objectives for which the organization is set up. The following journal entries may be made to incorporate the above information in the accounting system of a NPO.

1. For services rendered by the NPO to the society,

   Services to society a/c ......DR.
   To Service and Sacrifice a/c.

   (Being the amount of services rendered to the society).

2. For sacrifices made by the funding agencies :

   Services and sacrifices a/c.....DR.

   To Sacrifices by the funding agencies.

   (Being the sacrifices made by the funding agencies).

3. For Sacrifices made by the employees associated with the organization :

   Service and sacrifices a/c .... DR.

   To Sacrifice made by the employees.

   (Being the sacrifices made by the employees through rendering services to the society).

4. For sacrifices made by the organizers :

   Service and sacrifice a/c .... DR.

   To Sacrifices made by the organizers.

   (Being the excess of services generated over the sacrifices made by the funding agencies and the employees i.e. the sacrifices made by the organizers).

The above entries, it incorporated in the accounting system of these NPOs in memorandum form, will make the financial reporting mode informative. This will, in fact, be used by the resource providers and others in making rational decisions.

Here a question may arise : where should the social surplus created in a NPO should be transferred ? In income and expenditure account of a NPO it is found that the excess of income over expenses or the excess of expenditure over the income merges ultimately with ownership capital or capital fund, as the case may be. But in case of services and sacrifice account of a NPO, the surplus or services over sacrifices need not be transferred to any capital fund account, for such surplus does not represent any wealth. In fact, it is already consumed by the beneficiaries of the entity who are practically the members of the society.

Balance Sheet : Now comes the balance sheet. A Balance Sheet in an accounting system shows the financial position of an entity by detailing the different sources of funds (i.e. equities and liabilities) and the utilisation of these funds (i.e. assets). In other words, it presents the assets and liabilities of an entity in an articulated manner.

An Asset has the following characteristics :

(i) The organization should legally enforceable claim on it.

(ii) The organization should own it so that it can control the asset.

(iii) It should be possessed by the entity with the expectation of deriving services from it in the future.[7]

Liabilities and equities on the contrary, represent the amount of obligations to outsiders which arise from transactions or other events of the entities and the value of ownership of the assets under the control of the entity.

Human resources are at the heart of an organization and in case of NPOs, we cannot think of a welfare organization where the associated people do not volunteer their services. In the true sense of the term, employees of NPO cannot be considered under the ownership control of the entity. It also cannot be supposed that an entity have legally enforceable claim on them. But it is expected that the entity will have the opportunity to enjoy the services in the future as before[8] from these HRs who will stay with the organization. Only on this count they may be considered valuable resources to the entity and also to the society. That is why they are termed as assets. So, the people of NPOs should be valued and reported which is not done on the conventional financial reporting. The balance sheet as said earlier, would be more useful if such information is provided an addition to what is usually provided in such statements.

However, presentation of assets in the balance sheet of a NPO raises some knotty problems. In the traditional accounting system physical and monetary assets at the disposal of an entity are shown in the assets side of the balance sheet. Questions generally arise : How should the human resources be valued ? How should such values, it valued, be recorded in accounts ? If they are recorded as assets (i.e. application of fund) what should be considered the source (i.e. fund) of such resources ? In other words what should be the counterpart of such assets in the liability side of the balance sheet ?

The question how the HRs should be valued has already been discussed in detail in chapter two. There the Lev-Schwartz model, because of the circumstances of the case, is suggested for application to our study. Answers to the other two questions are discussed below.

The HR value represents the embodiment of the social equity while the total of physical and monetary assets signifies the capital fund of the organization. Since value of HRs are considered as wealth to the entity it may naturally be assumed that there are some people who are to own and enjoy the same. In this context the society in general may be assumed to be the owner of such wealth and this is why value of HRs are shown as assets and similar amount has been posted in the opposite side as 'social equity'.

Moreover, the position of HRs in relation to other assets can present an interesting picture of the organization. For instance, it may be usually found that the ratio between other assets and HR assets is much higher in case of POs than that in case of NPOs. This ratio seems to be of very interesting and useful to the funding agencies and investors for evaluation of performance of HRs of the entity. In NPOs, higher the ratio between HR and other resources, better should be considered the performance of the organization. Hence such a system of presentation and accounting may provide an index of asset structure of these entities. Anyway, a pro-forma of a balance sheet of a NPO may be presented as below (Table-11).

Table-11

Balance Sheet (incorporating HR value) of ...
As at ... ...

Liabilities	*Rs.*	*Assets*	*Rs.*
Capital Fund	***	Physical Assets	***
Social Equity	***	Monetary Assets	***
		Human Resource Assets	***
	***		***

III
Ways to Appraise the Performance of NPOs

The persons associated closely with an organization, whether it is a profit seeking one or non-profit seeking one, are very much interested in the information on the overall as well as individual group performance obtained to attain the objective of the organization. How can we assess the performance of a NPO ? At the first stage we are to measure the market value of series rendered to the society and the market value of services the employees provide to the entity. Once we can have an estimate of the two, we are in a position to draw up Service and Sacrifice Account as designed earlier. Then we are to value the sources of such services, that is, we are to value the HRs and draw up the balance sheet. How these items are to be valued are discussed in chapter five and six. As we have already designed the service and sacrifice Account and the Balance Sheet incorporating the HR value, we can develop same ratios with the help of which we can evaluate various matters like relative sacrifices of funding agencies, employees and organizers, relative efficiency of physical and monetary assets and human resources etc. Thus we can evaluate the relative performance of a NPO. If the performances of a few NPOs with similar activities are analysed compared and evaluated over the years, a trend of the services rendered by an organization can be identified. Moreover, the funding agencies will also be able to analyse the comparative efficiencies of NPOs where they are requested to contribute. An analysis of the various ratios may serve the above purpose.

The financial ratio analysis, it is a fact, is one of the most powerful tools in the hands of decision makers for assessing the financial strengths and weaknesses of a firm by establishing properly a relationship between the items of the Balance Sheet and the Profit & Loss Account. To quote Metcalf and Titard, "Analysing financial statements is a process of evaluating relationship of the component parts of financial statements to obtain a better understanding of a firm's position and performance".[9]

When we want to examine the financial performance of NPOs, the following ratios in line of the profit seeking organizations may be taken into consideration.

Table-12
Pyramid of Ratios
Return on Investment (ROI)
Net Service to Society

Conventional assets[10]+ HR assets

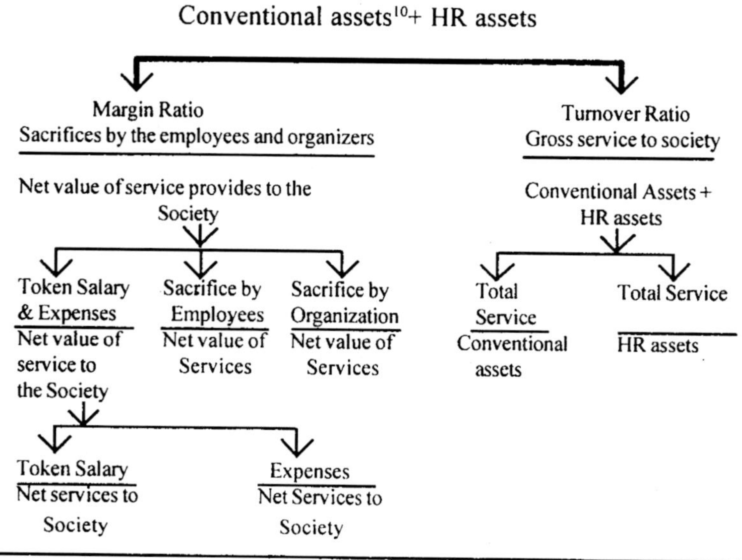

Source : G.C. Sinha, Op.cit, p. 148.

Let us interpret the above ratios to infer an inter-relation among various accounting parameters as drawn up earlier. Here the ratios are similar to those drawn on POs.

A. **Return on Investment :** In addition to its identification as the benefit a accruing to the owners the net profit is considered as an index of managerial performance[11] The ratio is considered to show the rate of return on capital invested by the owners. It is computed as :

$$\frac{\text{Net Profit (before interest and taxes)}}{\text{Owned capital or total assets}}$$

As this ratio signifies the index of managerial efficiency, various authorities use it to often for deciding on various issues on the funds invested in an organization. While the higher ratio denotes the success of the organization in attaining its objectives, the lower ratio, on the other, indicates the inefficiency of management.

In case of NPOs, a similar ratio may be drawn as below :

$$\text{Return on Investment} = \frac{\text{Net service to society}}{\text{Conventional assets + HR assets}}$$

Here neither the entity nor the contributors is interested in the magnitude of services provided to the society in relation to the total assets (including HR assets) under the disposal of the organization.

As in the case of POs, this ratio can be treated as an index of performance of NPOs. The contributors also can use this ratio to come to a conclusion whether they will continue to contribute in favour of a organization or not. The numerator of the ROI ratio signifies the profit earned by the profit seeking organizations, whereas in case of NPOs this ratio will indicate the net services rendered to the society. The denominator, in both cases, however, represents the investment or resources used to earn profit or to render service, as the case may be. Net results in both the cases, signify the performance of the organizations.

However, the ratio in case of NPOs, is subject to some limitations. It is difficult to calculate the total assets (which comprises of the conventional assets and also the HR assets, as per our proposed model) in an objective manner. While the conventional assets can be easily determined, the valuation of HRs is very contentious. However, it may be observed that if the ratio is calculated, taking into consideration the HR value, the information will be more informative and useful to the decision makers.

B. **Margin Ratio :** This ratio may be computed as :

$$\frac{\text{Gross Profit}}{\text{Sales}}$$

Since profitability of a firm, in case of profit seeking organization, depends ultimately on sales margin (i.e. the surplus of sales over the cost of sales), the ratio is considered most important for financial analysis.[12] The more the margin, the more the profitability. This ultimately determines the survival of the entity. A higher rate of profit margin on sales is also a sign of efficient management that minimizes the cost of production resulting in sufficient return to the owner's equity.

The margin ratio in case of NPOs can be presented as below :

$$\frac{\text{Sacrifices by the employees and organizers}}{\text{Net value of services to the society}}$$

Here, net value of services to society implies the excess value of services rendered over the collection from the beneficiaries. The ratio signifies the contributions or sacrifices made by the employees and organizers of an entity per rupee of net services provided to the beneficiaries. With the help of this ratio, in NPOs the degree of contribution of the employees in particular, and the organization in general, in relation to net value of the services can be identified. Like the index of managerial efficiency of POs, this ratio may be considered as an index of performance of NPOs. A higher ratio generally implies greater efficiency in performance of the organizations in achieving the desired goal.

C. **Turnover Ratios and Turnover Velocity :** Turnover ratios are used to indicate how effectively the assets have been utilised.[13] This is why it is called the activity ratio or assets management ratio. In business enterprises, efficient use of assets are measured through comparing them with sakes. The ratio may be computed as below :

Turnover ratios - (i) $\frac{\text{Sales}}{\text{Capital employed}}$

(ii) $\frac{\text{Sales}}{\text{Fixed assets}}$

(iii) $\frac{\text{Sales}}{\text{Debtors}}$ etc.

The higher the turnover ratio, grater the efficiency in the utilisation of the assets in debt and credit management.

In the parlance of NPOs, similar ratios in the following form can be drawn.

Turnover ratios - (i) $\frac{\text{Gross value of services to beneficiaries}}{\text{Conventional assets}}$

(ii) $\frac{\text{Gross value of services to beneficiaries}}{\text{Conventional assets + HR assets}}$

(iii) $\frac{\text{Gross value of services to beneficiaries}}{\text{HR assets}}$

These ratios may assist the subscribers in evaluating the effective use of assets or resources vested with the entity. Higher the value of the ratios, greater the efficiency in utilising the assets. An establishment with higher turnover ratios will get preference to others while the donors consider to allocate their funds to various welfare organizations.

D. **Operating Ratio :** In profit seeking organizations, operating ratio, i.e. ratio between cost of goods sold to sales is used to denote how much of per rupee of sales is necessary to run the operation.[14] Higher the ratio less the surplus is left to be utilised as profit. In other words, less the ratio, higher is the operating income.

A similar ratio may be drawn for a NPO. Here operating ratio can be drawn as below :

$$\frac{\text{Salary paid to the employees \& other expenses}}{\text{Net value of services to the beneficiaries}}$$

The ratio can reveal how much of the value of services generated by the entity is necessary to meet the expenses for running the organization. The reciprocal of the ratio indicates the value of services to the beneficiaries per rupee of operating expenses.

Higher this reciprocal, greater should be considered the efficiency of the organization. This reciprocal provides an index of operating efficiency of the entity. Naturally an unit with lower operating ratio will draw the attention of the funding agencies, since it implies higher productivity capacity of the organization. Hence the organization will take necessary steps to economize the operating expenses so that the grantors may provide resources at higher rates.

E. **Expenses Ratio :** This ratio is calculated for analysing the profitability and the operational efficiency of a firm. An organization, whether it is a profit seeking or a non-profit seeking, incurs various operating expenses for its performance. Accordingly, the rate is computed by dividing expenses incurred to the sales made by the organization.

$$\text{Expenses Ratio :} \quad \frac{\text{Expenses}}{\text{Net Sales}}$$

As a working proposition, a low value of this ratio rather than its high value is always desirable to the management. A high expenses ratio implies a relatively small share of sales is available for meeting the financial liabilities of the entity. Through this ratio, the management can take preventive measures to reduce the operating expenses which ultimately leads to their better performance. In other words, it shows the ability of the management in controlling the expenses. However this ratio may not always be considered so important to the owners and contributors of the firm.

In case of NPOs, a similar ratio can be derived as below :

$$\frac{\text{Token Salary + Expenses}}{\text{Net Value of Services rendered to society}}$$

Here, the expenses in profit seeking organization refer to the various operating expenses borne by these entities for their operation. The expenses in NPOs generally include the token salary paid to those service-minded people and the payment to the suppliers of goods and services. The higher value of this ratio implies a lesser volume of services rendered to the society and vice versa. The NPOs, through this ratio, can take suitable measure to economize their pendings. Funding agencies, it may appear, may not be much interested in this ratio because they may be interested only about the quantum of services rendered to the society. But for evaluating the cost structure of a NPO, this ratio is of much use.

F. **Asset - Turnover Ratio :** In profit seeking organizations this ratio is used to denote the effective use of resources in relation to sales (i.e. turning over the assets in the form of sales realisation).[15] Such ratio may also be calculated in relation to individual types of assets separately. Usually fixed assets and working capital turnover ratios are computed to gauge the effective use of these assets. These ratios also denote the profitable use of the resources.

The important lacuna is that the ratio may sometimes give misleading information. For instance, an old and established company may have higher ratio of assets turnover in comparison to new organization, when its fixed assets are valued at historical cost and they are net of depreciation. The situation is not so grave in NPOs, since fixed assets here constitute a small fiaction of the total of physical, monetary and human resources.

In NPOs, similar ratio may be drawn to evaluate the effective use of the resources vested to the organization. The following ratios may be drawn :

Total assets turnover : $\frac{\text{Net value of services}}{\text{Value of assets}}$

Physical assets turnover : $\frac{\text{Net value of services rendered}}{\text{Physical assets}}$

Monetary assets turnover : $\frac{\text{Net value of services rendered}}{\text{Monetary assets}}$

Human resource assets turnover : $\frac{\text{Net value of services rendered}}{\text{Human resource assets}}$

These ratios may be used to examine how effectively these assets were used to generate the services. These ratio indicate the velocity of each group of assets under the disposal of the entity. Higher the value of these ratio, greater the capability of the organization of use such resources.

G. **Structural Ratios :** Ratios necessary to indicate efficiency in the generation of services and the efficiency in the use of assets have been discussed so far. But ratios may be computed to appraise the structural relations between the various assets, between assets and funds (i.e. among sources of such assets, funds and liabilities). These ratios are similar to balance sheet ratios of the profit seeking organizations.

As an example, a ratio may be drawn to reveal the structural relation between conventional assets and human resources.

Ratio of Conventional Assets to Human Resource Assets : This ratio has much significance to the NPOs, as it may assist in making a comparative analysis between the conventional assets and HR assets of the organization. In comparison to profit seeking organizations the HR value of NPOs should be much higher than the other conventional assets, for the HRs constitute the pivotal position of every NPOs. Hence, lower the ratios, more the HRs, more the prospect of deriving services from them for the benefit of the hapless people. The funding agencies should consider this point for evaluating the prospect of a NPO.

Although the HRs in NPOs are indispensable, the performance of other assets cannot be ignored. Because it is not possible by the HRs to render services without the help of physical and monetary assets. The conventional assets though occupy a small fraction of total assets of such organization, effective use of them also need scrutiny.

IV

A Comprehensive list of Ratios :

Analysis of financial statements through ratios is very much essential for sound decision making for the outsiders (e.g. investors, creditors, bankers etc.). Various financial ratios are used to analyse and interpret accounting reporting of an organization. We have discussed earlier a few of them considering their applicability to both POs and NPOs. This section attempts to provide a list of probable ratios which may be applied to NPOs for better understanding of accounting of those entities. These ratios can be categorised under three heads :

(a) Service and Sacrifice (similar to Revenue) Statement Ratios.

(b) Balance Sheet Ratios.

(c) Balance Sheet and Service & Sacrifice (Revenue) statement ratios.

Service & Sacrifice Statement Ratios

	Ratio	Components
1.	Margin Ratio	$\frac{\text{Sacrifice by the employees and organizer}}{\text{Net value of services.}}$
2.	Operating Ratio	$\frac{\text{Token Salary + Expenses}}{\text{Net value of services.}}$
3.	Efficiency Ratio	$\frac{\text{Sacrifice by employees and organization}}{\text{Net value of services.}}$
4.	Token salary to net value of services rendered to society	$\frac{\text{Token salary}}{\text{Net value of services rendered}}$
5.	Expenses (excluding salary) to net value of services rendered	$\frac{\text{Expenses}}{\text{Net value of services rendered}}$

	Ratio	Components
6.	Sacrifice of the employees to net value of services rendered	$\frac{\text{Sacrifice by employees}}{\text{Net value of services rendered}}$
7.	Sacrifices of the funding agencies to net value of services rendered	$\frac{\text{Sacrifice by funding agencies}}{\text{Net value of services rendered}}$
8.	Sacrifice of the organization to the net value of services rendered	$\frac{\text{Sacrifice by the organization}}{\text{Net value of services}}$

Balance Sheet Ratios

	Ratio	Components
9.	Conventional assets to total assets	$\frac{\text{Conventional assets}}{\text{Physical assets + human resource assets}}$
10.	Human resource assets to total assets	$\frac{\text{Human Resource assets}}{\text{Physical assets + HR assets}}$
11.	Physical assets to human resources assets	$\frac{\text{Physical assets}}{\text{Human resources assets}}$
12.	Organization equity to social equity	$\frac{\text{Organization Equity}}{\text{Social Equity}}$
13.	Social equity to total assets	$\frac{\text{Social Equity}}{\text{Total assets}}$
14.	Organization Equity to total assets	$\frac{\text{Organizational Equity}}{\text{Total assets}}$

Balance Sheet and Service & Sacrifice Statement Ratios

Ratio	Components
15. Return on Investment	$\frac{\text{Net value of service}}{\text{Physical assets + HR assets}}$
16. Turnover Ratio	$\frac{\text{Gross value of service}}{\text{Physical assets + HR assets}}$
17. Physical assets turnover	$\frac{\text{Net value of services}}{\text{Physical assets}}$
18. Human resource assets turnover	$\frac{\text{Net value of services}}{\text{Human resource assets}}$
19. Net value of services to physical assets	$\frac{\text{Net value of services}}{\text{Physical assets}}$
20. Net value of services to human resource assets	$\frac{\text{Net value of services}}{\text{Human resource assets}}$
21. Sacrifice by employees to physical assets	$\frac{\text{Sacrifice by employees}}{\text{Physical assets}}$
22. Sacrifice by employees to human resource assets	$\frac{\text{Sacrifice by employees}}{\text{Human resource assets}}$
23. Sacrifice by organization to physical assets	$\frac{\text{Sacrifice by organization}}{\text{Physical assets}}$
24. Sacrifice by organization to Human resource assets	$\frac{\text{Sacrifice by organization}}{\text{Human resource assets}}$
25. Sacrifice by funding agencies to physical assets	$\frac{\text{Sacrifice by funding agencies}}{\text{Physical assets}}$
26. Sacrifice by funding agencies to Human resource assets	$\frac{\text{Sacrifice by funding agencies}}{\text{Human resource assets}}$

Ratio	Components
27. Donations to organization equity	$\frac{\text{Donations}}{\text{Organizations' Equity}}$
28. Donations to social equity	$\frac{\text{Donation}}{\text{Social Equity}}$

Users of the Ratios

The questions may arise : Who are interested in these ratios ? Do these ratios provide any guideline to the interested parties ? These may be discussed here briefly in the following way.

1. **From Donor's angle :** The funding agencies may find the following ratio useful :

$$\frac{\text{Net value of service rendered}}{\text{Total donations received from donors}}$$

This ratio is the reciprocal of donation and subscriptions received to total services provided to the society. The funding authorities through this ratio, may have some idea about the performance of the organizations and about the efficiency of the organization in utilising the funds in generating and distributing such services.

This ratio, therefore, indicates the services generated per rupee of donations granted to the organization.

2. **From Employee's angle :** The personnel who have volunteered their services to the organization may also be desirous of evaluating their performances in the generation and distribution of services to the society. The following ratio may provide such information to these interested people.

$$\frac{\text{Net value of services rendered}}{\text{Value of employee's sacrifice}}$$

The higher the ratio, the greater is the proportion of sacrifice by these people. The reciprocal will indicate the value of the service rendered to the society per rupee of their sacrifice.

3. **From the Angle of the Society :** The society as a whole may be interested in knowing the volume of services generated per rupee of sacrifices made by the associated employees and the organizers. The donors may want to learn about the effective use of their donations. The society barring the donors. On the other, is interested in the information on the magnitude of services consumed by the hapless people. This can be identified by the following ratio.

$$\frac{\text{Sacrifice of the employees and the organizers}}{\text{Net value of service generated}}$$

The reciprocal of the same may be used to indicate the value of services to the beneficiaries per rupee of sacrifices of the employees and organizers.

4. **From Organizer's view :** The organizers always want to maximize services that can be rendered to the beneficiaries per rupee of expenses incurred, because the ultimate goal of these NPOs is to generate and distribute as much services as possible to the society. The following ratio may be used for the purpose :

$$\text{Expenses Turnover Ratio} : \frac{\text{Net value of service to the beneficiaries}}{\text{Expenses incurred}}$$

The ratio indicates value of services per rupee of expenses. In other words it may be considered as an index of efficient use of money spent for running organization. Higher the ratio, more fruitful the expenses.

V

Conclusion

A large number of other ratios based on the proposed model can be computed to have an in depth study about the performances by a welfare organization. But model building is one thing and applying it to

7. E.L.S. Hendriksen, *Accounting Theory*, Richard D. Irwin, 3rd edition, 1977, pp. 257-258.

8. Rensis Likert, *The Human Organization : Its Measurement and Values*, McGraw Hill, New York, 1967, pp. 84-95.

9. Metcalf, R.W. and P.L. Titard, *Principles of Accounting* (Philadelphia) 1976. W.B. Saunders, p. 157.

10. Conventional assets refer to total of physical assets and monetary assets.

11. Robert F. Meigs & Walter B. Meigs, *Financial Accounting*, Analysis and interpretation of financial statements, McGraw Hill Book Co. 1989 Ch. 15, pp. 575-614.

12. Prasanna Chandra, Financial Statement Analysis, *Financial Management Theory and Practice*, Tata McGraw Hill Publishing Company Limited, New Delhi, 1990, Ch. 8, p. 133.

13. Prasanna Chandra, "Financial Statement Analysis," *Financial Management Theory and Practice*, Tata McGraw Hill Publishing Company Limited, New Delhi, 1990, Ch. 8, p. 132.

14. Gordon Shillinglaw, Gordon and Ronen, "Financial Statement Analysis," *Accounting : A Management Approach*, Richard D. Irwin, Inc, Homewood, Illinosis, 6th edition, 1979, Ch. 17, p. 332.

15. G.A. Lee, "Analysis and Criticism of Published Financial Statements," *Modern Financial Accounting*, ELBS, 1983, 3rd edition, Ch. 18, p. 410.

5

Application of the Proposed Accounting Model to a Nonprofit Organization

Introduction

In order to overcome the limitations of the traditional accounting system of the NPOs in presenting in the financial reports the magnitude of services rendered by the entity, the value of the efforts of the people who render such services and the sacrifices of the organizers for the same, an accounting model has been developed to supplement the conventional accounting system. In this chapter an attempt has been made to find out how far the proposed model works. For this purpose a voluntary organization namely, the Rama Krishna Mission Boys' Home, Rahara, West Bengal, India has been selected. First its objectives and various activities, its management, sources of finance are discussed in brief. Subsequently, why this charitable unit is so indispensable to the local people are discussed here in brief. Next to it, the Annual Report containing 'A/C Hospital and Dispensary' and the 'Balance Sheet' as prepared by the organization is presented in order to highlight how the funds are collected, the way they are used, the various assets the entity holds and the liabilities i.e. obligations the entity is to meet. The fourth section deals with the measurement problems relating to various components of the proposed model. The various assumptions considered in detailing the different components of the proposed model are discussed in the subsequent section. Next to it is presented the proposed 'Service and Sacrifice Account' which is drawn on the basis information collected for the purpose.[1]

With the help of some of the ratios, as devised in the earlier chapter, the components of the account have been analysed to make an appraisal of the performances of the entity. But appraisal of performance cannot be claimed to be complete unless the sources of such performance i.e. the concerned HRs are evaluated. That is left for the next chapter.

I

Rama Krishna Mission Boys' Home

A Brief History : After the sad demise of Sri Ramakrishna Paramhansha Dev, the great Hindu prophet of the 19th Century in India, August 1886, his disciples, under the leadership of Swami Vivekananda, formed a monastic brotherhood which in due course developed into, Ramakrishna Math. The fundamental attribute of the organization is to provide 'service to mankind', irrespective of caste, nationality and colour. With the view to spreading over the ideology of Sri Ramakrishna Dev and demonstrating the truth in real life, Swami Vivekananda in May 1897, founded the Ramakrishna Mission.

The Headquarter of Ramakrishna Math and Ramakrishna Mission is located at Belur. The place is in the district of Howrah and is about six Kilometers away from Calcutta on the western bank of the Ganges. Later in course of time the organization through its multifarious social services acquired international fame. Its dimensions of rendering services have extended to many corners of the World through its various branches. The Ramakrishna Mission Boys' Home, Rahara (RKMBHR) is one of such branches.

Location : The foundation stone of the Home was laid on 16th August, 1944. Late Swami Punyanandaji Maharaj, a senior monk of the Ramakrishna order, was its first secretary. The Home is located in the rural surroundings at Rahara, a village about 20 kilometers away from Calcutta, on the eastern side of the Khardah Railway Station on the Sealdah-Ranaghat Section of Eastern Railway of India.

Management : The management of the Home is controlled and guided by the headquarter of Ramakrishna Mission at Belur. The Governing Body of the organization appoints a management committee for controlling the operation of the organization. The committee is generally comprised of both monastic and other members of the organizations. The managing committee then with the approval of the Governing Body of the Mission appoints various sub-committees to look after the operation of different branches. Swami Jayananda, is present Secretary of RKMBHR.

Objectives and Activities : The RKMBHR is a religious charitable institution and provides services for the benefit of the general public. 'Service to mankind' is their sole motto. Although this organization performs a leading role in imparting education, they also provide medical services to the public of the locality. A hospital and a charitable unit are run by the institution for providing medical services. Where the hospital is exclusively meant for the residents of Ashrama, the charitabale unit is for providing services to whoever comes.

Imparting education is most important objective of R K M B H R. There are 13 educational units where both orphan and outside students are provided education at various levels beginning from basic to post-graduate education. From among the orphan boys who do not have much aptitude for formal education are offered opportunity for learning vocational trade such as tailoring, carpentary, bakery, poultry, book-binding etc. so that when they leave the Home they can earn independently without making him a burden to the society.

The Home also extends their helping hands to local people and also others when they are in distress during flood, epidemic and various other natural calamities.

Finance : The organization operates exclusively on Government grants, tuition fees from students and the donations from generous members of the public, philanthropics, charitable trust etc. During 1990-91 the Home has maintained about 700 orphans, destitute and adibashi boys entirely free of any charge. A part of their food, clothings, medical care, entertainment is satisfied from its own resources and donations while the other part is met by a per capita grant of Rs. 255/- received from the Government. But during these days of increasing prices every year the Home had to cope with a huge deficit. This deficit were met through the donations received from different sources. The Home provides various other services depending primarily on the contributions received. Because of the spiralling increase in price of all commodities it has to depend more and more on such donations.

The various activities performed by the Home through its different units may be summed up below :

A. **Educational Activities :** One of the most important objectives of RKMBHR is to impart education to the students. The students can be categorised under three headings : (a) Ashrama Scholars, (b) Hostel Scholars, both of whom reside within the campus and (c) Day-Scholars who live with their parents. While the former gets education at free of cost the latter two have to pay the requisite tuition fees.

The basic objective does not confine to imparting education, but it extends to providing them training in such manner that they may grow into healthy, self-disciplined youngmen with a sound moral foundation.

The various education units of the Home are :

(a) Prebasic (Nursery) School

(b) Junior Basic School

(c) Junior High School

(d) High School

(e) Junior Technical School

(f) Higher Secondary Vocational Institute

(g) Primary Teachers' Training Institute

(h) Brahmananda Post-Graduate Basic Training College

(i) Work Education Training Centre

(j) Ramakrishna Missions Vivekananda Centenary College

(k) District Library and Mobile Library Service Unit

(l) Librarianship Training Centre

(m) Audio Visual Unit.

B. **Non-Educational Activities :** Apart from providing education to students, the Home also provides training on printing, tailoring, book-bindings etc. to those orphan students who are not capable of formal education. They are provided such training so that they become self-supported and they would not be treated as burden to the Society. The non-educational training is provided through the vocational school. The Unit is comprised of the following departments :

(a) Diary

(b) Backery

(c) Poultry

(d) Carpentary

(e) Tailoring

(f) Plumbing

(g) Book-binding

(h) T.V., Radio, Tape recorder repairing.

C. **Medical Service Units :** The medical services by the Home are provided through two separate units maintained for such purpose. They are :

(a) Hospital, and

(b) Charitable Unit.

Particulars on them are presented below.

The Hospital : The Home runs a hospital. The monks, orphans, the large number of teaching and non-teaching staff associated with the entity usually avail themselves of the opportunity. Here treatment of ordinary illness and simple surgical operations are usually carried on. In emergency the Home, however, makes arrangement for their critical treatment by removing them to a more modern equipped hospital, namely, the Ramakrishna Mission Seva Pratisthan, a Unit controlled by the headquater of Ramakrishna Mission. It is worth-mentioning here that the hospital maintained by RKMBHR is attended by qualified and distinguished medical practitioners as Honorary Visiting Physicians. These doctors provide services either voluntarily or receive a token remuneration from the Home. There are also assistants and ward-boys who assist the doctors, look after the patients in absence of the physicians and carry out their directions. In this unit there are two such doctors who pay regular visit to the patients here.

The Charitable Unit : Besides the hospital, the Home also provides medical services to the public through its charitable unit. The unit is comprised of a general department. That apart, there are eye department, ENT department and a dental department. These departments are also attended by specialist physicians who either receive nothing or take a token amount for their services. These doctors come two days a week and spends four hours to examine the patients. A token amount is collected from these patients. While Rs 5.- are charged for treatment of eye, Rs. 2/- are charged for treatments in other departments per patient per visit.

Both the hospital and charitable units are controlled by a committee appointed by the RKMBHR sub-committee. They generally make arrangements for appointing specialised doctors to provide services to people. The number of patients to be treated during a period are not usually estimated in advance. But the basic goal of the unit is to provide medical service to the poor. The extent of services that can be rendered depends heavily on the grants and contributions available from Government and other agencies.

Therefore finance is a vital factor here. Generally, more the fund, it is expected, more capable is the entity in rendering services. The Government makes a special grant to the Home exclusively for the medical services. But the amount is so meagre in comparison to the expenses incurred for providing such services that Home is to arrange for making good the huge deficit of the charitable unit. It is met by the Headquarter out of its general fund. For instance in RKMBHR, out of the total expenses Rs. 67,386/- incurred for such medical services (both in hospital and charitable unit, vide Income and Expenditure Account in appendix I) a sum of Rs. 7,665/- is received as a token fees from the patients of charitable unit, Rs. 19,700/- is received as a grant from the Government and the Balance of Rs. 40,021/- is compensated by the Home from other sources of contributions. Therefore, the Home is continuously running year after year with deficit which has accumulated to an alarming figure of Rs. 3,33,305/- (vide Balance Sheet Appendix - II).

II

Need for the Charitable Unit to Local People : Question generally arises, why this charitable unit is so indispensable to the people of the locality ? Or what purpose does this serve to make itself so necessary ?

It may be mentioned here that most of the inhabitants of the area migrated from East Pakistan (presently Bangladesh) after partition of India and Pakistan. India is a poor country with purely an agricultural-based economy. The people who emigrated from Bangladesh during the middle of 1940s are basically poor. Although in recent days with the advancement of technology there is a slight improvement in the standard of living of these people, a major portion of them still are economically backward. These people have no other alternative but to struggle with their limited resources to live. For them diseases are part and parcel of their lives. Hence they are in need of basic medical services. Such services, although available, in the local market are usually out of their reach.

Moreover, unlike other developed countries, there is no wide spread provision of medical insurance in India. Hospital are generally run by the Governments. But the capacity of these hospitals is very limited to provide the facilities to all the citizens. In such a situation, the people here are to make their own arrangement of treatment according to their economic ability.

The economically backward people and also the middle class suffer the most. They neither have the facility to treat in the hospital nor can afford to pay the huge amount as fees charged by the nurshing homes and also the private practitioners. Consequently, these people depend very much on the services of the charitable unit run by the RKMBHR. Because of these reasons this unit is so indispensable to these people.

III

Annual Accounts of the Home: A Sketch of the annual accounts of these two units derived from the annual reports of the organization is represented below. The detail of the Income and Expenditure Account as published by the organisation is given in Appendix - I. Items of incomes and expenses are presented here under some broad heads (vide Table 13 and 14).

TABLE 13

R. K. Mission Boys' Home, RAHARA

A/c. Hospital and Dispensary*

Income & Expenditure Account for the Year Ended on 31.03.1991

To	Establishment pay & allowances	42,612[1]	By	Government grants and other donations	27,365[6]
"	Hospital & Other Medical expenses	17,097[2]	"	Deficit	40,021
"	Repairs & Renewals	1360[3]			
"	Office & Administrative expenses	5,776[4]			
"	Miscellaneous expenses	541[5]			
		67,386			67,386

* The organization (RKMBHR) uses this title in their financial report. Explanation of the items (i.e. 1,2,3...12) are made in the following pages.

TABLE 14

Balance Sheet

LIABILITIES		ASSETS	
Building fund less depreciation	33,119[7]	Building fund less depreciation	29,442[10]
Furniture and Equipment fund less depreciation	12,277[8]	Furniture and Equipment fund less depreciation	17,142[11]
Transfer from Rama Krishna Mission General Fund (2,94,472 + 40,021)	3,34,493[9]	Accumulated deficit (2,93,284 + 40,021)	3,33,305[12]
	3,79,889		3,79,889

1. Establishment pay & allowance are comprised of :

		Rs.	
General Department	-	30,515.00	
Dental Department	-	3,000.00	
Eye Department	-	2,400.00	
ENT Department	-	3,000.00	
Homeopathy Department	-	2,400.00	
Puja Allowance	-	925.00	
P.F. Contribution	-	372.00	Rs. 42,612.00
		=	Rs. 42,612.00

2. Hospital & other Medical Expenses are comprised of :

Diet charges	-	15,127.50	
Washing charges	-	238.00	
Medical expenses	-	994.49	
Bedding & Clothing	-	250.00	
Hospital Utensils & equipments		487.00	Rs. 17,096.99
		=	Rs. 17,097.00

3. Repairs and Renewals :

General Repairing	-	11.00	
Repairs of the building	-	1,249.44	Rs. 1,360.44
		=	Rs. 1,360.00

4. Office and Administrative expenses are comprised of :

Electric charges	-	4,957.55	
Stationery & Printing	-	177.30	
Travelling expenses	-	62.00	
Audit fees and expenses	-	235.00	
Postage & Telegram	-	344.00	Rs. 5,775.85
		=	Rs. 5,776.00

5. Miscellaneous expenses :

Contingencies (General)	-	526.25	
Contingencies (Homoeopathy)-		2.20	
Clearing and sanitation	-	12.25	Rs. 540.70
		=	Rs. 541.00

6. Government grants and other donations are comprised of :

Government grants	-	19,700.00	
Donations	-	7,665.00	Rs. 27,365.00
		=	Rs. 27,365.00

Balance Sheet

Liabilities

7. Building Fund less depreciation :

Building Fund (as per last Balance Sheet)	- .	34,669.07	
Less Depreciation	-	1,549.60	Rs. 33,119.47
		=	Rs. 33,119.00

8. Furniture and equipment fund less depreciation :

Furniture and equipment Fund (as per last Balance Sheet)	-	14,181.38	
Less Depreciation	-	1,904.70	Rs. 12,276.68
		=	Rs. 12,277.00

9. Transfer from Rama Krishna Mission General Fund :

As per last Balance sheet	-	2,94,472.10	
Add during the year	-	40,020.98	Rs. 3,34,493.08
			= Rs. 3,34,493

Assets

10. Building Fund less depreciation :

Building Fund (as per last Balance Sheet)	-	30,992.00	
Less depreciation @ 5%	-	1,549.60	Rs. 29,442.40
			= Rs. 29,442.00

11. Furniture and equipment fund less depreciation :

Furniture and equipment fund (as per last Balance Sheet)	-	19,047.00	
Less depreciation @ 10%	-	1,904.70	Rs. 17,142.30
			= Rs. 17,142.00

12. Accumulated deficit :

As per last Balance sheet	-	2,93,283.55	
Add excess of expenditure over income	-	40,020.98	Rs. 3,33,304.53
			= Rs. 3,33,305.00

The Figures here vide Appendix - I & II of RKMBHR.

For the benefit of calculations the amounts are rounded off (to the nearest rupee)

It may be observed that the above accounts present information on the grants received under different heads, collections from the patients, and the payments on medical expenses, and the amount of deficit contributed by the parent body. This account is, therefore, capable of presenting the sources of financing the annual expenditure and the ways how such finances are used. In fact, the account reports how the management use the resources according the restrictions imposed by the granting authorities (in this case the parent body).

But does it speak of the extent of services rendered to the poor ? Does it indicate the extent of sacrifices of the people associated with the organization? Can we infer something about the productive use of the resources vested with the entity? These bits of information cannot be derived from the above accounts. The above accounts has its necessity, no doubt, as it indicates the stewardship performance of the management, but it cannot report the extent of the unit's performance. In other words, users of this statement cannot have an idea about how far the objective for which the entity is established has been achieved. Hence, it appears that the basic objective of accounting to report on the annual performance of an entity does not materialise here.

Now, let us make an humble attempt to apply to the present situation to our accounting model developed in the earlier chapter. But application of the model involves the following measurement problems.

IV

Measurement Problems Relating to Various Components of the Model : Every measurement system is based on certain assumptions. For instance, in case of traditional accounting system usually nothing is recorded in the books of accounts unless that is supported by exchanges or transactions. The other assumption is that the surplus or deficit of wealth arising from the activities accrues ultimately in favour of the owners. Another assumption is that the entity will continue for an indefinite period. These assumption hold good to business enterprises. But in case of NPOs excepting the third assumption, the other two have a little relevance.

It is fact that, as per the first assumption, the records should be based on transactions or exchanges so as to provide an objective measurement of various elements. In such cases there is little scope for personal judgement. But in case of welfare organization the extent of welfare provided is not valued in the market through exchanges. Hence, an objective measure of the same is not available. This is the crux of the problem. We should design a system to quantify the welfare content of the activities, otherwise our main objective of measuring and reporting the performance of a welfare organization will be frustrated. To minimise the controversy we should take certain steps. For instance we are to quantify the services first in non-monetary terms, say, the numbers of patients treated, the number of days they stay in Hospital for treatment, the number of doctors employed in the organization, the nature of services rendered i.e. patients attended, surgical operation done etc. Next, we are to determine the market value of those services. But market value of such services may not be available always. In such cases we are to depend on other alternative sources from where we can derive an estimate about the value of the services. Estimation on the extent of services and their values are influenced by subjective elements and accordingly they are controversial. But it provides an idea about the trend of the achievement of a welfare organization.

Keeping in mind the above limitations in the measurement of the elements of the model, we may try to quantify the following components :

(a) Value of services rendered to the society (SS).
(b) Value of sacrifices of the employees (W^2).
(c) Value of the contribution generated by the organization (O).

In fact the value of services provided by the organizers is residual in nature, because it will be determined by deducting the contribution of the donors and the employees from the value of services rendered to the needy public. Hence our problem centres around to the measurement of the first two components i.e. SS and W^2.

For measuring the market value of services rendered to the society (SS) we have considered the following into account :

1. First, the information on the number of patients to whom such services are provided in the hospital and the charitable unit, and the types of services rendered to these patients has been collected.

2. Then have been considered the market value of similar services provided by the Polyclinics or Nursing Homes situated in the locality. For the purpose we have taken information in the fees charged by three of such organizations. Although the facilities given are more or less equal, there exists a slight difference in charges from nursing home to nursing home. The rates used here are based on the information provided by the professional physicians attached to the hospitals nursing homes and polyclinics of the locality (vide appendix - III and IV). The process is followed for different types of treatment made there.

3. Then we are to multiply the rate per patient per treatment by the numbers of patients treated in individual groups. By adding all the figures thus arrived at, of the different treatments, we get the total value of services rendered and from the value is deducted the token collection received from the beneficiaries treated in the charitable unit of RKMBHR to get of SS (vide Appendix - VI).

As to the valuation of sacrifices made by the employees (W^2) the following steps have been taken.

1. First, the number of doctors, attendants, ward boys etc. employed in the organization and their stay with the Home per day per week have been determined (vide Appendix VIIa).

2. Next, the rate of valuating the above services is estimated by collecting information on the rate of pay made to those employees rendering similar services in the similar position in the Government hospitals of the locality (vide Appendix VIIb).

The rate is multiplied by the services rendered to the society to get the market value of the services of the employees. From the product is deducted the token salary paid to them to get the sacrifice of the employees (W^2) (vide Appendix - VIII).

An important point is worth mentioning here. Price lists of the various kinds of services rendered to the needy people is not available, because such services are not considered like standards goods. Hence, we are to depend on information collected through interviews. But the main limitation of such system is that, there is a scope of inflating or deflating the actual figures. Notwithstanding, it provides an idea on the issue.

Now the measurement of the elements in terms of money is in order.

V

Application of the Proposed Accounting Model : With a view of applying the accounting model to the charitable institute, let us measure first the individual components of the model. For this purpose the services generated by the organization to the society is represented by the value of 'P' which is the market value of services charged by any other medical service unit having an intention to earn profit (vide Appendix-VI)*. The nominal charges collected from the patients of charitable unit is shown in Appendix - V. Information on the amount of donation and payment of salaries to staff are obtained from the Annual Accounts (vide Appendix - I). How the values are collected is shown below :

SS = Social Surplus represented by the excess of market value of services rendered to the society (P) over the token collection made from the beneficiaries (Q).

Where, P = The services generated to the society by the NPO, which is similar to the market value of services charged by any other welfare organizations having a motive to earn profit (vide Appendix - VI)

= Rs. 5,86,150

Q = Token collection from the direct beneficiaries arrived at as (number of patient attended the charitable unit X nominal charges per individual fixed by the respective unit). [vide Appendix - V]

= Rs. 7,665.

Therefore, SS = P - Q

= Rs. 5,86,150 - Rs. 7,665

= Rs. 5,78,485 [vide Appendix - VI].

* Hospitals in India are run by Governments or Public bodies. Here patients are usually treated free of cost. Most of the people of India are not under the cover of medical insurance. Hence, in the underdeveloped economy like India, the common people are to depend on these hospitals. Here, doctors, nurses, attendants are government employees and their remuneration may be used as standard.

Again, SS = SS = F (D, W^2, O)

Where, D = Contribution made by the donors, or

D = G + W_1 - Q

Here, G = Payment too supplier of goods and services, which represents the aggregate of hospital & other medical expenses, repairs & renewals, office and administrative expenses and miscellaneous expenses incurred by the organization for the functioning of its two welfare units (vide Appendix - I & Table 13 of page 125).

= Rs. 17,097 + Rs. 1,360 + Rs. 5,776 + Rs. 541

= Rs. 24,774.

W_1 = The token payment to those dedicated persons associated with the organization under the heading 'Establishment pay and allowances' (vide Appendix - I).

= Rs. 30,515 + 3,000 + 2,400 + 3,000 + 2,400 + 925.00 + 372.00

= Rs. 42,612.00.

Therefore, D = G + W_1 - Q

= Rs. 24,774 + Rs. 42,612 - Rs. 7,665

= Rs. 59,721 [representing part of the total sacrifices made by the funding agencies].

Again, W_2 = The sacrifice made by the dedicated persons, which can be arrived as the difference between the actual salary paid as per our Government rule, comprising of basic, D.A. house rent allowance and medical allowance and the token salary paid to them (W_2) by the institution (vide Appendix - VIII).

= Rs. 3,12,181 (representing part of the total sacrifices made by the service minded people).

And O = The sacrifice made by the organizers or NPO itself, which is arrived as [O = SS - (D + W_2)], i.e. the surplus of the value of services generated and distributed (SS) to the people of the society over the sacrifices made by the fundings agencies (D) and the employees (W_2) of the organization.

= Rs. 5,78,485 - (59,721 + 3,12,181)
= Rs. 5,78,485 - 3,71,902
= Rs. 2,06,583 (vide Appendix - IX).

VI

Now let us put the above value in service and sacrifice Account of welfare organization (Table - 15).

TABLE 15

Services and Sacrifice Account of Ramakrishna Mission Boys' Home, Rahara for the Year Ended on 31.3.1991

	Sacrifices of benefactor	*Rs.*	*Rs.*		*Services to beneficiaries*	*Rs.*	*Rs.*
1.	Sacrificing of the funding agencies (D)			4.	Social services rendered (SS)		
	Payment to supplier of goods and services (G)	24,774			Market value of social services (P)	5,86,150	
	Add : Token payment to dedicated employees (W_1)	42,612			Less : Token collection from beneficiaries (Q)	7,665	
	($G + W_1$)	67,386			[P - Q = SS]		5,78,485
	Less : Token collection from beneficiaries (Q)	7,665					
	[($G+W_1$-Q) = D]		59,721				
2.	Sacrifice made by the employees (W_2)		3,12,181				
3.	Sacrifice made by the organization (O)		2,06,583				
			5,78,485				5,78,485

TABLE 16

Balance Sheet (Redrafted) of Ramakrishna Mission Boys' Home, Rahara as on 31.3.1991

Liabilities	*Rs.*	*Rs.*	*Assets*	*Rs.*	*Rs.*
Specific Funds			**Physical Assets**		
Building	33,119		Building	29,442	
Furniture	12,277	45,396	Furniture	17,142	46,584
Capital Fund			**Monetary Assets**		-
Balance	3,34,493		**Human Resource Assets**		-*
Less : Accumulated deficit	3,33,305	1,188			
Social Equity		-*			
		46,584			46,584

* The social equity signifies the human resources assets of the organization. As the value of HRs are not considered here, the value of social equity is not shown in this chapter. It is shown in the next chapter.

VII

Performance appraisal with the help of the accounts : Efficiency of an activity can be revealed distinctly through the study of the rate of outcome per unit of effort. In case of NPO, the effort is made by the donors, employees and organizers. The outcome is the net social services rendered to the needy people. Efficiency in the use of the fund, the rate of contribution of the employees, and the organizers and the service generating ability of the entity as a whole can be revealed through some of the ratios developed in chapter four. Here some of those ratios are calculated to apprise the performance of the organization.

1. **Margin Ratio :**

The ratio can be arrived as :

$$\frac{\text{Net service } (W_2+O) \text{ or sacrifices by employees and organization}}{\text{Net value of services rendered (SS)}}$$

$$= \frac{\text{Rs. }3,12,181 + \text{Rs. }2,06,583}{\text{Rs. }5,78,485}$$

$$= \frac{\text{Rs. }5,18,764}{\text{Rs. }5,78,485}$$

$$= 0.90 : 1$$

It refers to the margin of the net value of services over the related expenses. Here, the net value of service to society, as discussed earlier, implies the surplus of market value of services to society over the token charges received from the beneficiaries, which the net service represents the aggregate of services of the employees and the organizers. The ratio implies how much of the net value is contributed by the employees and the organizers. Here, the ratio comes to 0.09 : 1. That means, donors contribute only 10% of the value of the services generated by the organization. In other words, with the help of the employees and organizers, the donor's grant can create services valuing ten times of the donation. Higher the ratio, it may be inferred, greater the efficiency of the organization in accomplishing the objective of NPO. An organization with higher margin ratio will automatically be preferred to other by the funding agencies.

2. **Operating Ratio :**

Similar to operating ratio in POs, a ratio may be computed. Here the basic objective is to reveal how much of per rupee of net value of service rendered is used to meet operating expenses like salaries and other expenses. The ratio will be as follows :

$$\text{Operating Ratio} = \frac{\text{Total Salary + Expenses } (W_1 + G)}{\text{Net Value of social services (SS)}}$$

$$= \frac{\text{Rs. }42,612 + \text{Rs. }24,774}{\text{Rs. }5,78,485}$$

$$= \frac{\text{Rs. }67,386}{\text{Rs. }5,78,485}$$

$$= \underline{0.12 : 1.}$$

In RKMBHR only 12% of the net value of services rendered is utilised for payment to employees and the suppliers of goods necessary for providing services. Implication of high operating ratio is that operating expenses constitute only a small fraction of the Net Value of Social Services rendered to the Society. This ratio serves as a weapon in the hands of the donors to measure the operational efficiency of an organization for providing services.

Reciprocal of this ratio (i.e. $\frac{\text{Rs. } 5{,}78{,}485}{\text{Rs. } 67{,}386} = 8.58 : 1$) indicates that per rupee of expenses, net social services worth Rs. 8.58 are generated. More the value of this reciprocal, higher the productivity of the resources. It may be considered as an index of effective use of resources.

3. **Salary Service Ratio :**

Ratio of salary to employees to the net value of services rendered may be computed to indicate how much of the net value of services is used to pay the salaries of the employees. Here ratio is as below :

$$\text{Salary service ratio} : \frac{\text{Salary to employees } (W_1)}{\text{Net value of services (SS)}}$$

$$= \frac{\text{Rs. } 42{,}612}{\text{Rs. } 5{,}78{,}485}$$

$$= 0.07 : 1.$$

The ratio here comes to 0.07 : 1. This means per rupee of social services only seven paisa are paid to the employees. The persons associated with the organizations on whole-time basis are very poorly remunerated. Part-timers also serve almost voluntarily against token remuneration. It may be interpreted that volunteered services are indispensable in such type of social work.

4. **Employee's Sacrifice to Social Service Ratio :**

Ratio between the sacrifice of people of the NPO and the net value of services rendered to the society may be revealed by the following ratio :

$$\text{Employee sacrifice to social service ratio} = \frac{\text{Sacrifice of employees } (W_2)}{\text{Net value of services (SS)}}$$

$$= \frac{\text{Rs. } 3,12,181}{\text{Rs. } 5,78,485}$$

$$= 0.54 : 1.$$

The extent of sacrifice of the employee is highlighted through this ratio. Higher the ratio, greater will be the service received by the society. For RKMBHR, the ratio is 0.54 : 1. An organization having less of this ratio, may be interpreted as that its employees are paid at higher rate, in relation to service rendered to the needy people. That means employee's contribution there for the cause of the poor is not so high. The ratio may be considered as a rough and ready indicator of the service mentality of the employees.

5. **Donors' Sacrifice to Social Service Ratio :**

Ratio between sacrifice by the funding agencies and the net value of services rendered may be determined by the following ratio :

$$\text{Donors' sacrifice to Social Service Ratio} = \frac{\text{Sacrifice by the funding agencies (D)}}{\text{Net value of services (SS)}}$$

$$= \frac{\text{Rs. } 59,721}{\text{Rs. } 5,78,485}$$

$$= 0.10 : 1.$$

The ratio here comes to 0.10 : 1. That means, of the total services generated by the organization, the funding agencies contribute only 10%. In other words the ratio reveals how much per rupee of net value of services is rendered by the contributors and donors. Although, out of the three categories of persons involved in these organizations, the funding agencies sacrifice the minimum, their contributions are of immense importance for providing services and for the existence of the entity as well. However, through this information the funding people may have an idea of their involvement and can react accordingly.

Reciprocal of the ratio (i.e. $\frac{5,78,485}{59,721}$ = 10 : 1) indicates that per rupee contribution of the funding agencies it is expected, more will be the magnitude of services. This ratio also signifies the effective use of funds of the contributors.

6. **Organizers' Sacrifice Service Ratio :**

Ratio between sacrifices of the organizers to net value of services may be drawn to indicate the degree of contribution of the organizers. This may be called organizers' sacrifice service ratio. It may be drawn as below :

$$\text{Organizers' Sacrifice Service Ratio} = \frac{\text{Sacrifice by the organizers (O)}}{\text{Net Value of services (SS)}}$$

$$= \frac{\text{Rs. }2,06,583}{\text{Rs. }5,78,485}$$

$$= 0.36 : 1.$$

The ratio comes to 0:36:1. This may be used as a barometer of the organizer's ability and skill. It reveals how efficiently the organizers can co-ordinate various sections of the society for the cause of the needy people. The ratio shows that even if the employees are paid at the market rate, the organizers can generate more than one-third of the net value of services only with the administrative ability. Higher the ratio, greater the efficiency of the organizers. Hence the granting authority may use the ratio as an index of the capability of the organizers of the welfare units.

VIII

Conclusion

Now, let us examine how far the objective of accounting for the NPO (as discussed in Chapter Three) has been achieved. Since the basic objective is to measure and report the performance in terms of organization's identified goals, the information of net value of services rendered serves the purpose. As regards the effective use of the resources, information derived through the margin ratio, employees sacrifice service ratio etc. may provide an helpful idea. The contributions of various groups of people associated with the organization can also be inferred from the ratios discussed above. These information has their limitations. They may be called conjectural, arbitrary and subjective. Despite such limitations, the fact cannot be denied that the service sacrifice account provides an indication as to the magnitude of performance of the organizers.

From the above discussion it is further revealed that, three categories of people are involved in the NPOs to achieve their desired goal. They are :

(a) The organizers
(b) The funding agencies ; and
(c) The associated people who are running the day to day activities.

When involvement of these people are observed, the role of the organizers comes to our notice first, because without their brain and labour these organizations could never see the light of the day. In other words, they provide the platform from where the other two can get the opportunity to act. Next come the funding authorities. An organization without money is helpless. It is the funding agencies who extend their helping hands by supplying funds without the expectation of getting any return. The last category of the people who are the most important are those dedicated people who complete the run by making the process moving.

A comparative analysis on the performance of these three reveals that of the total service generated, the organizers provide 36% and the funding agencies serve 10%, while the employees contribute the major portion of 54%. It is fact, that because of the active participation of people -- donors, employees and organizers -- the services are generated. But all of the three cannot be considered the resources of the organization. In POs, the organizers (i.e. the management) are considered responsible for earning the surplus (i.e. profit). But in the literature on HRs they are not considered human resources perhaps on the grounds, that they are not contemplated to be controlled. That apart, it is absurd to think of spending money for their recruitment and development. But in welfare organizations, the contribution of the organizers, in general and the monks in particular are invaluable. Attempts can be made to measure them. But that is an area of further investigation.

Hence, remains the employees, it is found from the analysis that 54% of the social services come from the sacrifices of the employees. Thus, these people are the primary source of such services. Value of their services rendered, during an accounting period, are measured and reported in Service and Sacrifice Account. But the source of stock of such services should be valued and reported in the annual accounts. An humble attempt to this end has been made in next chapter.

Reference

1. The Service and Sacrifice Account and the Balance Sheet, presented here is based on the figures available from the audited report of the organization (Vide Appendix I). The Balance Sheet after incorporation the HR Assets, the object of our study, will be discussed in the next Chapter.

6

Valuation of Human Resources of A Charitable Unit as per Lev-Schwartz Model

Introduction

Selfless employees of the welfare organizations who volunteer their labour for the cause of the poor are the fountain of these services rendered to the society. Our problem is to quantify the value of such sources to the entity and to report the same in the annual accounts of the organization. As discussed in Chapter two, there are various models to account for HRs. But all of them cannot be used for our purpose. Some methods require to capitalise the historical cost of recruitment, training and development of HRs, some methods need to determine the cost of replacing existing employees for the purpose. Some other methods aim to calculate the opportunity cost of the services of the existing employees. These methods assume perhaps, that employees are to be selected from a competitive labour market and that the departments within an entity are in competition to use the services of individual employees. But the case in NPOs is quite different because here the employees are selected on the basis of their willingness to volunteer their services for the cause and betterment of mankind. In some other models like economic valuation method, return on efforts employed method, value measurement method and non-monetary method, the extent of expected services, efforts given by individual employees, their earnings for next 5 years, management skill, labour participation etc. are to be quantified. These methods appear logically sound. But measurement of them is too difficult to provide an objective assessment of human resources. They are not even applied to profit seeking organizations. In most of the empirical studies so far done, the Lev-Schwartz model is used. It is so because it is easy to collect data required for the purpose and it emphasizes on the capitalised value of remuneration payable to the employees. Since salaries are determined through agreements, measurement of HRs value becomes easier. In case of NPOs, it is fact, salaries paid to the employees do not represent the market value of their services. Notwithstanding, market value of these services can be determined through collecting information on the value of the employees providing similar services, in profit seeking organization. This is why, the study aims to quantify the value of HRs of that organization as per the Lev-Schwartz model.

For this purpose, here a detailed analysis on the Lev-Schwartz model comprising of various variables and the method of deriving information on them have been discussed first. Assumptions taken to quantify the variables and the problems faced to measure them are discussed later on. Subsequently, Balance Sheet, incorporating the HRs value has been drawn. Then, with the help of some ratios proposed in the earlier chapters the financial strength, effective use of resources, extent of achieving the objective of the organization etc. have been appraised.

I

Lev-Schwartz Model

The value of an employee, according to the authors,[1] is determined by aggregating the present value of the wages and salaries which an employee can earn during his stay with the organization. The measurement of the value of HRs can be done by adopting the following formula :

$$V_{\lambda} = \sum_{t=\lambda}^{T} \frac{I(t)}{(1+r)^{t-\lambda}}$$

Where, V_{λ} = The human capital value of a person ' λ ' years old.

λ = The year when the employee joins the organization.

T = The person's retirement age.

I (t) = The person's annual earnings upto retirement.

r = A discount rate specific to a person.

For empirical verification, the terms used in the model need some clarification. They are discussed here in brief.

II

Measurement Issues

1. Here 'T' represents the person's retirement age i.e. the age when a person normally retires from his service. As we consider the hospitals and charitable institutions of a welfare organization, for our study, we should consider the retirement age used in government institutions. Here, the employees retire at the age of 60 years. In our study we find the normal retirement age to be 65 years on the ground that aged professional physicians and superannuated people are generally keen to serve these institutions (It is evident from investigation).

2. 'I (t)' represents here the series of annual earnings of an individual upto his retirement. The assumption being that an employee will serve these organizations upto the date of his retirement without any changes in his positions. That means, he will not think of any promotion. The other assumption being, the employees will stick to these organizations. In other words, the possibility of labour turnover or early retirement and similar factors are not considered here. Here the earnings are based on the pays and allowances as per the government orders.

3. 'r' refers to the discount rate applicable to specific persons. It appears that different rates will be used to discount the salary of the individuals according to the nature of importance of the employed individuals. Here, it is assumed that all the persons are of equal importance to the institution and hence a single rate is used.

Now, the question generally arises, how should we determine the rate of interest for discounting the series of services expected to be derived from the personnel. Here a number of interest rates should be considered for the purpose. For instance, we should include the rates of interest on savings account in a bank on fixed deposits, on public deposits collected by the companies, rate of interest charged by the bank in banking loan, bank discount rate fixed by the Reserve Bank of India etc. In this case, though there are so many alternatives, the rate of interest on fixed deposits with a nationalised bank[2] should be treated as representative because here the risk element is minimum and the liquidity of the investment is not very high.

III

Valuation Process : The valuation process of an individual (here the professional physician) can be described here in brief (vide Appendix VIIc). An example may serve the purpose. Dr. S. Banerjee, who has been serving selflessly RKMBHR hospital, provides 3 effective hours per day for 6 days a week for attending the patients (like the doctors in the government hospitals). He is approximately of 60 years of age on the date of measuring the value and has 5 more years to render his service. Had he been in State Government health service, his pay at his age, as per the government rules, would have been Rs. 8,557 p.m. and Rs. 1,02,684 per year (calculation of total salary of the doctors and attendants are discussed in Chapter Five) (vide Appendix VIIb and VIIc respectively.) By discounting the total salary of Dr. S. Banerjee @ 15% for 5 years the present value of his earnings comes to Rs. 3,44,217 (vide Appendix X). Likewise, Dr. P. Roynandi, as for another example, provides one effective hour of service per week of 18 effective hours. His imputed earnings per year will be proportionately less because he provides less period of service than Dr. S. Banerjee in the hospital. Accordingly, by discounting his annual earnings from the unit comes to Rs. 4,043 [i.e. $\frac{\text{Rs. 6,005 x 4 x 12}}{72}$ = Rs. 4,043, since his normal salary per month as a whole is Rs. 6,065 [vide Appendix - VIIb & VIIc]. The capitalised value of the earnings will be the HR value of the individual to the organization. The value of the other doctors and attendants engaged in this hospital and charitable unit are determined accordingly. The sum of these values represent the total HR value of the organization [vide Appendix X]. This amount is shown in the Balance Sheet on the assets side as the social equity on the liability side, since society is considered as the owner of such assets [Table - 18].

The balance sheet, both under the traditional accounting system (as presented by the RKMBHR) and also by incorporating the human resource value are shown in the next page.

TABLE 17

Rama Krishna Mission Boys' Home, Rahara
A/c. Hospital and Dispensary
Balance Sheet* (Under Traditional System) as on 31.03.1991

Liabilities	Rs.	Assets	Rs.
Building Fund Less depreciation	33,119	Building Fund Less depreciation	29,442
Furniture & Equipment Fund less depreciation	12.277	Furniture and Equipment Fund less depreciation	17,142
Transfer from Rama Krishna Mission General Fund (2,94,472 + 40,021)	3,34,493	Accumulated deficit (2,93,284 + 40,021)	3,33,305
	3,79,889		3,79,889

*(vide Appendix - II)

TABLE 18

Rama Krishna Mission Boys' Home, Rahara
A/c. Hospital and Dispensary
Balance Sheet (as per the proposed model and incorporating human resource value) as on 31.03.91

Liabilities	Rs.	Rs.	Assets	Rs.	Rs.
Specific Funds			**Physical Assets**		
Building	33,119		Building	29,442	
Furniture	12,277	45,396	Furniture	17,142	46,584
Capital Fund			**Monetary Assets**		
Balance	3,34,493				
			Human Resource Assets		17,93,486*
Less : Accumulated deficit	3,33,305	1,188			
Social Equity		17,93,786			
		18,40,370		18,40,370	

*(vide Appendix X)

Some Observation

Following points should be kept in mind while studying such statements :

1. Less the proportion of physical and monetary assets, in relation to the value of human resources, more should be considered the possibility of rendering services to the society.

2. The magnitude of monetary assets alone should not be considered here the indicator of solvency. Suppliers of goods or services usually do not treat these balances as to the security of their dues. Hence, these organizations generally hold little balance in this account. In otherwords, whatever is received is utilised for providing services to the society. It is natural expectation that funding agencies will provide resources to meet the dues to the suppliers.

3. The value of human resources is shown in the assets side and its counterpart is shown in the liability side as the social equity of the organization, since the society alone can claim the ownership of such resources.

4. The total value of physical and monetary assets equal to the aggregate of specific and capital funds of the non-profit organization.

5. Donors, it is expected, should donate where the proportion of HRs in relation to other assets are relatively high. Such organizations are expected to generate greater volume of services and hence that will help the society in a much better way.

IV

Interpretation of the Statements (Service and Sacrifice Account and Balance Sheet) Through Ratios

Information on HRs of a NPO, particularly in respect to charitable units, may help us in analysing its performance with the following ratios :

1. **Position of HR assets in relation to total assets** may be known from the following ratio.

$$\text{Ratio of HRs to total assets} = \frac{\text{Value of Human resources}}{\text{Total assets}}$$

$$= \frac{\text{Rs. } 17{,}93{,}786}{\text{Rs. } 18{,}40{,}370}$$

$$= \underline{0.97 : 1}$$

Here the ratio is 0.97 : 1. In other words, physical assets, monetary assets and other conventional assets constitute only 1/32th of HR value. Higher the value of the ratio, greater should be considered the existence of selfless people in the organization for the benefit of the society. The funding agency may consider the ratio as an index of the existence of permanent and valuable source of social services at the disposal of the organization. They should be more generous to an entity which holds high proportion of HRs. In this case it is 97%. If another organization whose HRs constitute less than the proportion and where other things remain the same, the granting authority would not prefer that organization to others for granting funds.

2. **Role of physical assets to total assets** may be revealed from the following ratio.

$$\text{Ratio of physical assets to total assets} = \frac{\text{Value of physical assets}}{\text{Value of physical assets + HR assets}}$$

$$= \frac{\text{Rs. } 46.584}{\text{Rs. } 46{,}584 + \text{Rs. } 17{,}93{,}786}$$

$$= \frac{\text{Rs. } 46{,}584}{\text{Rs. } 18{,}40{,}370}$$

$$= \underline{0.03 : 1.}$$

The conventional assets represent only 3% of the total of these assets and human resources. In these organizations the performance of

HRs are very important, although the role of physical assets can not be oversighted. Higher the value of the ratio, it should be inferred, less the scope of receiving services from HRs. The funding agencies are interested in those organizations which have greater human resources for rendering social services.

3. **Intensity of HRs in relating to contributions from donors** may be inferred from the following ratio.

$$\text{Ratio of HRs to donations and grants} = \frac{\text{Value of human resources}}{\text{Annual contribution of the funding and other agencies}}$$

$$= \frac{\text{Rs. } 17{,}93{,}786}{\text{Rs. } 67{,}386}$$

$$= \underline{26.6 : 1}$$

Here the ratio is 26.6 : 1 The ratio may be considered similar to economists idea of capital intensity[3]. It is an indicator of the capital value of HRs per rupee of input of donation. Higher the value of ratio, more the value of the people associated with the charitable unit. In case RKMBHR it is 26.6 : 1. If in another NPO, it is less than this figure, it may be inferred that RKMBHR makes more efficient use of resources because of their human forces.

4. **Effective use of HR capital** may be examined through the following ratio.

$$\text{Ratio of HRs to services rendered} = \frac{\text{Value of Human resources}}{\text{Net value of services rendered to society.}}$$

$$= \frac{\text{Rs. } 17{,}93{,}786}{\text{Rs. } 5{,}78{,}485}$$

$$= \underline{3 : 1}$$

Here the ratio is 3 : 1. The ratio may be considered similar to economists' capital-output ratio[4], which indicates the value of HRs per rupee of net services rendered to the society. It is an index of the efficient use of HRs of an entity. Higher the value of the ratio, higher should be considered the efficiency of the employees. In RKMBHR the ratio is 3 : 1. In other way of speaking, HRs worth Rs. 3 creates social services of Re. 1. If in another case, it is less than the rate of Re. 1, it may be inferred that the latter is not as efficient as the former.

5. **Rate of sacrifice of employees** may be revealed through the ratio of the value of their sacrifice to society to that of human assets of the entity. Here the ratio is as below :

$$\text{Ratio of Employees' sacrifice to human resources} = \frac{\text{Value of employees' sacrifice to society}}{\text{Value of Human resources.}}$$

$$= \frac{\text{Rs. } 3,12,181}{\text{Rs. } 17,93,786}$$

$$= \underline{0.17 : 1}$$

Here it is 0.17 : 1. It reveals the service rendering capabilities of the employees. Higher the ratio, greater will be the intensity of sacrifice of the employees of the organization. In RKMBHR the ratio is 0.17 :1. Another NPO with higher value of this ratio indicate that it has more dedicated people. Hence that organization will attract more attention of the contributors.

6. **Organizers' contributions in relation to HR capital** can be known from the following ratio.

$$\text{Ratio of organisers' contribution to HRs} = \frac{\text{Value of organizers' contribution to society}}{\text{Value of human resources}}$$

$$= \frac{\text{Rs. } 2,06,583}{\text{Rs. } 17,93,786}$$

$$= \underline{\text{Rs. } 0.12} : 1$$

Here the ratio is 0.12 : 1. It implies that per rupee of HR capital, approximately 12 paise of social services are created out of organizational activities. Higher the value of the ratio, it should be inferred, greater the capabilities of the organizers. In the unit under study, namely the RKMBHR (Hospital and Charitable unit), of the total volume of sacrifices rendered to the society, the employees contribute the major portion. Notwithstanding, the sacrifice made by the organization itself is not less important. This ratio may be considered an index of organizations' capability in relation to HR capital.

7. **Service generating capacity of the assets** can be revealed through the following ratio :

$$\text{Ratio of social service to total assets} = \frac{\text{Net service to society}}{\text{Physical assets + Human resources assets}}$$

$$= \frac{\text{Rs. } 5{,}78{,}485}{\text{Rs. } 46{,}584 + \text{Rs. } 17{,}93{,}786}$$

$$= \frac{\text{Rs. } 5{,}78{,}485}{\text{Rs. } 18{,}40{,}370}$$

$$= \underline{0.31 : 1}$$

This ratio may be considered to be similar to the return on investment ratio. Here the ratio comes to 0.31 : 1. It implies that per rupee of total assets, services worth 31 paise are rendered to the needy. This ratio may be treated as an index of effective use of the assets of the voluntary organization. Higher the ratio, it may be inferred, the more competent is the organization in achieving their objective of the rendering services to the society. It can also be assumed that an organization with higher value of this ratio will attract the attention of the donors in times of allocating funds to voluntary organizations.

8. **Physical and monetary assets turnover** may be ascertained through the following ratio.

$$\text{Physical and monetary assets turnover ratio} = \frac{\text{Net service to society}}{\text{Physical assets + Monetary assets}}$$

$$= \frac{\text{Rs. } 5{,}78{,}485}{\text{Rs. } 46{,}584}$$

$$= \underline{12.4 \text{ times.}}$$

With this ratio the donors can evaluate the effective use of the physical and monetary assets in generating services to the society. In RKMBHR these assets may be assumed to provide services which worth 12.4 times of value. Although the performance of these voluntary organization basically depends on the competence of the employees and organizers, role of these assets should not be under estimated. When an organization holds larger physical and monetary assets but generates less services, it may be interpreted that the unit as a whole is not efficient enough in extracting greater volume of services through these inanimate resources.

V

Some Ratios Based in HRA

Several other ratios may be drawn to analyse the performances and services rendering capacity of the organization. A few ratios are designed and discussed below.

1. Return on Investment $= \frac{\text{Net value of services}}{\text{Physical assets + HR assets}}$

$$= \frac{5{,}78{,}485}{46{,}584 + 17{,}93{,}786}$$

$$= \frac{5{,}78{,}485}{18{,}40{,}370}$$

$$= \underline{0.31 : 1}$$

2. Margin Ratio $= \dfrac{\text{Sacrifice by employees and organizers}}{\text{Net value of services}}$

$= \dfrac{3{,}12{,}181 + 2{,}06{,}583}{5{,}78{,}485}$

$= \dfrac{5{,}18{,}764}{5{,}78{,}485}$

$= \underline{0.09 : 1.}$

3. Turnover Ratio $= \dfrac{\text{Gross value of services}}{\text{Conventional assets + HR assets}}$

$= \dfrac{5{,}86{,}150}{46{,}584 + 17{,}93{,}786}$

$= \dfrac{5{,}86{,}150}{18{,}40{,}370}$

$= \underline{0.32 : 1.}$

4. Operating Ratio $= \dfrac{\text{Token salary + Expenses}}{\text{Net value of services}}$

$= \dfrac{42{,}612 + 24{,}774}{5{,}78{,}485}$

$= \dfrac{67{,}386}{5{,}78{,}485}$

$= \underline{0.12 : 1}$

5. Efficiency Ratio $= \dfrac{\text{Sacrifices made by employees and organizers}}{\text{Net value of services}}$

$= \dfrac{3,12,181 + 2,06,583}{5,78,485}$

$= \dfrac{5,18,764}{5,78,485}$

$= 0.90 : 1$

6. Conventional assets Turnover $= \dfrac{\text{Net Value of services}}{\text{Physical assets}}$

$= \dfrac{5,78,485}{46,584}$

$= 12.4$ times

7. Token salary to net value of services to society $= \dfrac{\text{Token salary}}{\text{Net value of service}}$

$= \dfrac{42,612}{5,78,485}$

$= 0.07 : 1$

8. Human resource Turnover $= \dfrac{\text{Net value of service}}{\text{HR assets}}$

$= \dfrac{5,78,485}{17,93,786}$

$= 0.32 : 1$

9. Expenses (excluding salary) to net value of services

$$= \frac{\text{Expenses}}{\text{Net value of service}}$$

$$= \frac{24,774}{5,78,485}$$

$$= 0.04 : 1$$

10. Sacrifices made by employees to net value of services

$$= \frac{\text{Sacrifice by employees}}{\text{Net value of service}}$$

$$= \frac{3,12,181}{5,78,485}$$

$$= 0.54 : 1$$

11. Sacrifices made by Organization to net value of services

$$= \frac{\text{Sacrifice by organization}}{\text{Net value of service}}$$

$$= \frac{2,06,583}{5,78,485}$$

$$= 0.36 : 1$$

12. Net value of service to society to physical assets

$$= \frac{\text{Net value of service}}{\text{Physical assets}}$$

$$= \frac{5,78,485}{46,584}$$

$$= 12.4 \text{ times.}$$

13. Net value of service of Human resource assets $= \dfrac{\text{Net value of service}}{\text{Human resource assets}}$

$= \dfrac{5,78,485}{17,93,786}$

$=$ 0.32 : 1.

14. Sacrifice by employees to physical assets $= \dfrac{\text{Sacrifice by employees}}{\text{Physical assets}}$

$= \dfrac{3,12,181}{46,584}$

$=$ 6.7 times

15. Sacrifice by employees to human resource assets $= \dfrac{\text{Sacrifice by employees}}{\text{Human resource assets}}$

$= \dfrac{3,12,181}{17,93,786}$

$=$ 0.17 : 1

16. Sacrifice by organization to physical assets $= \dfrac{\text{Sacrifice by organization}}{\text{Physical assets}}$

$= \dfrac{2,06,583}{46,584}$

$=$ 4.43 times.

17. Sacrifice by organization to human resource assets $= \dfrac{\text{Sacrifice by organization}}{\text{Human Resource assets}}$

$= \dfrac{2,06,583}{17,93,786}$

$=$ 12.0 : 1.

18. Physical assets to human resource assets $= \dfrac{\text{Physical assets}}{\text{Human resource assets}}$

$= \dfrac{46,584}{17,93,786}$

$= 0.03 : 1.$

19. Donation to organization equity $= \dfrac{\text{Donation}}{\text{Organization Equity}}$

$= \dfrac{67,386}{45,396 + 1,188}$

$= \dfrac{67,386}{46,584}$

$= 1.45$ times.

20. Donation to social equity $= \dfrac{\text{Donation}}{\text{Social Equity}}$

$= \dfrac{67,386}{17,93,786}$

$= 0.04 : 1.$

21. Organization equity to social equity $= \dfrac{\text{Organization equity}}{\text{Social Equity}}$

$= \dfrac{46,584}{17,93,786}$

$= 0.03 : 1$

22. Organization equity to total assets $= \dfrac{\text{Organization equity}}{\text{Total Assets}}$

$= \dfrac{46,584}{18,40,370}$

$= 0.025 : 1$

23. Organization equity to human resource assets $= \frac{\text{Organization equity}}{\text{Human resource assets}}$

$= \frac{46,584}{17,93,786}$

$= 0.03 : 1$

24. Social equity to total assets $= \frac{\text{Social equity}}{\text{Total assets}}$

$= \frac{17,93,786}{18,40,370}$

$= 0.97 : 1$

25. Physical assets to total assets $= \frac{\text{Physical assets}}{\text{Total assets}}$

$= \frac{46,584}{18,40,370}$

$= 0.03 : 1$

26. Human resource assets to total assets $= \frac{\text{Human resource assets}}{\text{Conventional assets + HR assets}}$

$= \frac{17,93,786}{18,40,370}$

$= 0.97 : 1.$

Various Groups and the Ratios of Their Interest

Let us point out through ratios the relative efficiency of the contribution of individual groups. For instance, donors are interested in the information of rate of service generated per rupee of their donations, and employees in the rate of services per rupee of their sacrifices. These issues may be pointed out with the following ratios.

27. Ratio of interest
from Donors' angle

$$= \frac{\text{Net services to society}}{\text{Donations \& subscription provided by donors.}} = \frac{5,78,485}{67,386} = 8.6 \text{ times.}$$

28. Ratio of interest
from employees' angle

$$= \frac{\text{Net service to society}}{\text{Sacrifice by employees}} = \frac{5,78,485}{3,21,181} = 1.85 \text{ times}$$

29. Ratio of interest
from society's angle

$$= \frac{\text{Net service to society}}{\text{Sacrifice by organization}} = \frac{5,78,485}{2,06,583} = 2.8 \text{ times}$$

30. Ratio of interest
from Organization view

$$= \frac{\text{Net service to society}}{\text{Total expenses incurred}} = \frac{5,78,485}{59,721} = 9.7 \text{ times}$$

Inter-relations among the ratios may be shown through the pyramid of ratios (see p. 144).

VI

Conclusion

In this chapter a humble attempt has been made to measure the value of people associated with RKMBHR as per Lev-Schwartz model. While applying the model for empirical study certain assumptions are taken into consideration and we have highlighted them in brief. Some other assumptions however may be considered for the purpose of such valuation. Therefore, there lies scope for further research to make the valuation process more logical.

Pyramid of Ratios

Return on Investment

$$\frac{\text{Net Service to Society}}{\text{Physical assets + HR assets}}$$

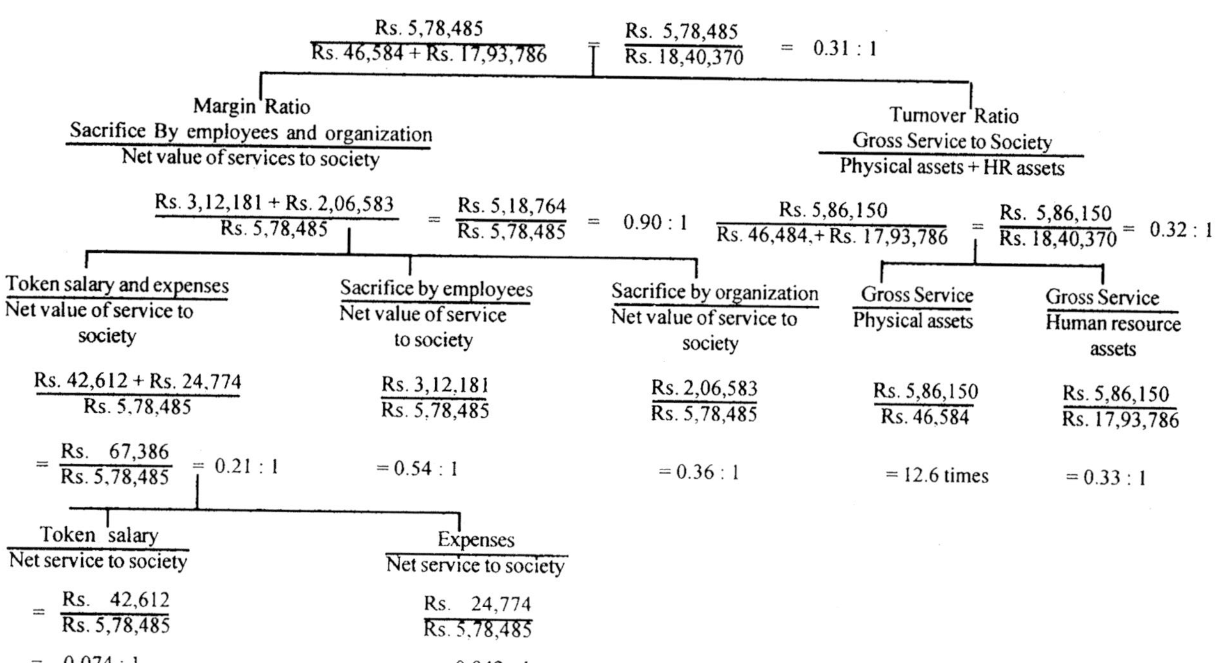

If HRA is introduced, it may be inferred that, information on the relative shares of HRs and other assets, the role of HRs in the organization, the performances of HRs and similar other issues can be derived. In absence of such HR valuation the related information will not be available for evaluating the relative performances of the non-profit organizations. Therefore, these bits of information, in addition to what is derived from conventional accounting system, it is expected, will help in evaluating the position of the organization in the society. More the value of HRs, higher the prospect of rendering services to the society. These bits of information, the author thinks, if supplemented with the traditional accounting reports, will help the different users of accounting information in deciding their allocation of resources among various welfare organizations. Notwithstanding a subjective element present in the measurement process, such a measure can be used to indicate the capabilities of an entity in terms of providing services to the society.

References

1. Baruch Lev and Aba Schwartz, "On the use of the Economic Concept of Human Capital in Financial Statements", *The Accounting Review*, Jan. 1971.

2. In India in the period of study this rate was 15%.

3. R.G. Lipsey, An Introduction to Positive Economics, ELBS, 1972, p. 230.

4. Thirlwall A.P., Growth and Development, with Special References to Developing Economics, ELBS, 4th ed. 1989, p. 117.

7

Summary and Conclusion

Introduction

Now let us sum up what we have done in the earlier Chapter. For the purpose, summary of the findings made in the previous chapters is presented here first. Subsequently, conclusion derived from such findings is described. The study ends stating the areas requiring further investigation.

One of the basic objectives of accounting is to report how far an organization's goal is realised. It requires the measurement of the performances of an organization and effective use of the resources under its control. Accounting system of profit seeking organization can meet these objectives, though to a limited extent, through Profit & Loss Account, Balance Sheet and other annual financial statements required for the purpose. But usually they do not measure and report the value of the HRs employed under such organizations. In case of NPOs, the problem is further aggravated. The accounting system here neither reports the achievements of the identified goals in terms of social welfare, nor reflects the value of the primary source from which the services rendered to the society flow out. This is why this study, as mentioned in Chapter one, evolves a system of accounting so that the basic goal for which the organization has been set up can be reflected, at least to some extent, in the annual accounting statements. But it requires (i) the measurement of the value to the NPO of selfless people associated with it[1] ; (ii) determination of the relative position of the value of HRs in comparison to other assets owned by the NPO[2] ;

(iii) quantification of the contribution made by the selfless people engaged in the NPO[3] ; etc. It was also mentioned that such information is necessary to evaluate the performance of the NPO in terms of accounting indicators and to determine the contribution made by the funding agencies of the NPOs in providing services to the society.

I

Summary

With a view to achieving these objectives, we are in need of measuring the services rendered to the society by the welfare organizations, the sacrifices made by donors, employees and organizers on the one hand, and the value of the basic source of such services (i.e. people associated with the NPO in particular) on the other. This is why, Chapter One has described the objective of the study, stated the research methodology adopted and outlined the scheme of the work.

For the purpose of valuing HRs of a NPO, we were in need of discussing major HRA Models developed so far. That has been done through survey of literature in Chapter Two. Salient features of these models were compared, analysed and appraised. On examination it was found that even though the models are sophisticated in concepts, application of all of them to our present study is not feasible due to paucity of information. The Lev-Schwartz model[4] , used by the few profit-seeking organizations, who have attempted to do so, across the world has been found to be suitable for our study.

Study of accounting system of a NPO sounds meaningless, if the existing commonly used accounting practices is not scrutinized. But accounting for welfare organization is not usually guided by enactments, laws or rules and regulations promulgated by the professional or similar authoritative bodies. As a result, the accounting model[5] commonly used (as published in Financial and Accounting Guide for Non-profit Organizations, 3rd ed. John Wiley & Sons, New York, and reported by Gross and Warshauer, partners Price Waterhouse) has been selected for our study. From the analysis it has been found that the system is designed to report the stewardship performance of an entity. In other words, it may be said that, the system is capable of reporting how far the restrictions imposed by the funding agencies have been observed in utilising the various funds entrusted to a welfare organization. But performance measures are not quantified in terms of organization's identified goals. But it should be the basic objective of accounting for a NPO (Trueblood Committee Report, Objective No. : 11). Hence, it may be inferred, the objective is not fully met.

To make up the shortcoming, the next Chapter i.e. Chapter Four, has attempted to develop a model[6] where the performances in terms of organization's identified goals can to some extent be assessed and reported. It has also attempted to identify the various sections of the society who contribute for the generation of such services. On scrutiny it has been found that the employees, the organizers with the help of the donors generate such services. Now comes the question of the relative importance of the contributors of such services. For the purpose some ratios[7] have been developed. This Chapter is primarily confined to establish theoretical foundation of the model. The next chapter is engaged to test the model through empirical evidence.

In Chapter Five, the basic objective was to measure empirically the value of the services generated by a welfare organization in a locality inhabited mostly by migrated poor people from East Pakistan (presently, Bangladesh). Though the locality lies within the suburban area of the city of Calcutta, in the province of West Bengal, India, the majority of the population are daily wage-earners who may expect themselves fortunate if they remain employed in one-quarter of a year. This is why, it is beyond their expectation to get the benefits of modern medical service as and when required. Under such circumstances the charitable dispensary run by the RKMBHR is of immense help to those hapless migrated people. In such cases, the cost of medicine in comparison to cost of other requirements for medical treatment is proportionately very low. Hence, the costs of services by the selfless professional physicians, attendants and office staff are not adequately represented in the traditional accounts. In fact, these people are indispensable for running such organizations. But the existing accounting system followed by the organizations portrary neither the value of their services, nor the value of those people associated to these organizations. Through interviews the quantum of services rendered to these hapless people and the market value of these services in the area have been determined. Once such values are quantified and they are put in the accounting format, it becomes easier to find out the contribution made by the organizers[8]. Afterwards, the contributions of the various sections, namely, employees, donors and organizers are analysed through ratios[9] and attempt has been made to gauge effective use of the resources donated by the granting authorities. Here margin ratio, operating ratio, salary service ratio etc. are computed to have a better understanding. In the unit under our study, the ratios are 0.9:1, 0.12 : 1 respectively. The margin ratio indicates the margin of social services over the financial cost incurred to obtain the service. In this organization the margin is 90%. The operating ratio refers to operating expenses to pay salary and cost of medicine per rupee of services. It is 12 paise per rupee of services. The salary service ratio is 0.07 : 1. It implies that cost of salary paid to the employees constitute only 7% of the net value of services rendered to the society. Other three ratios (i.e. employees' sacrifice to social services, donors' sacrifice to social service and the organization's sacrifice service ratio) represent the relative sacrifices of employees, donors and the organizers. In this organization the respective sacrifice are 54%, 10% and 36% of the net value of social services. These bits of information help pin point the relative importance of the people interested in these NPOs. The Services and Sacrifice Account of the unit clearly shows these issues. This account is capable of reporting only the flow of services received from the employees, but it does not quantify the value of the stock of such flow (as mentioned earlier) i.e. the value of human resources. That is discussed in next chapter.

Chapter Six, deals with the core of the problem. With a view to valuing the HRs, the main source from which the services originate, Lev-Schwartz model has been adopted. The various components of the model have been quantified on the basis of information collected through interview and other means[10]. The values of the services of these people, as prevailed in the nearby market i.e. in privately-run nursing homes, polyclinics and hospitals run by the government are considered as the basis of such valuation. Once such resources are measured the balance sheet is drawn incorporating such values[11]. Now, we are in a position to have a picture about the service generated, the sacrifices made by different sections of people, the value of the employees etc.[12]. These bits of information help us in making, though in a limited manner, the effective use of resources under the behest of the organizers. For instance, we may want to know the relative importance of HRs and physical and monetary assets in the organizations. It may be desired to derive a relation between the value of HRs and donation received and between value of HRs and those of net social services. In our present study HRs constitute 97% while the physical and monetary assets together represent the balance i.e. only 3% of the total assets. Again, per rupee of donation there are HRs valuing Rs. 26.6. It is worth mentioning to note that with how little amount of donation these persons try to serve the hapless people. As regards the effective use of HRs, it is evident that HRs amounting to Rs. 3 generate annually one rupee on net social services.

Analysis on the relation between sacrifices of employees and organizers to HRs provides an insight into the effective use of the resources. Here, per rupee of HRs, employees sacrifice 17 paisa, while organizers sacrifice 12 paisa. Besides, the relation between net social services and physical and monetary assets is a very important indicator as to the effective use of these assets. Here it is found that per rupee of these assets, the organization creates net social service worth Rs. 12.40. Greater the ratio, higher the return on the donor's contribution. It is a valuable index of efficient use of the organization's physical and monetary assets. Similarly, a number of other ratios has been devised to critically analyse the performance of the people of the organization in terms of its identified goals of creating social welfare.

II

Conclusion

Now let us conclude. Should the existing system of accounting be discarded ? The study does not propose so. It has been discussed earlier that contrary to earning profit, rendering of social service to the society, is the primary objective of NPOs[13]. The services again is generated primarily by the people associated with the organization with the help of the funds contributed by the funding agencies. But the existing accounting system is totally engrossed in representing how far the funds entrusted are utilised as per the restrictions imposed by the donors[14]. It is also observed that there is little scope of representing the value of HRs as well as value of services rendered by the various people associated with the organization. The information on the physical and monetary assets reported in the existing system cannot adequately speak of the achievements of the organization. Therefore, the accounting system of NPOs should be such as to give necessary information to the users. The proposed accounting system aims to serve the required purpose.

From the case study, it has been found that the physical and monetary assets constitute only 3% of the total assets, whereas the balance is represented by the HR assets of the organization[15]. This information is very much useful to the funding agencies to take rational decisions on future resource allocation. Moreover, of the total volume of service generated by the entity, the selfless people provided 56%. The organization contributed 34% while the donors contributed the balance[16]. The donors allocate their funds to the welfare organization not on the basis of their sound solvancy position. It is expected, they donate on the basis of the degree of dedication of the human forces associated to the entity. For instance, in the unit under study, the HRs comprise 97% of the total assets (i.e. aggregate of physical and monetary assets and HR assets). It is the portion of HRs that matters to the grantor. The value of other assets should not be considered so much important here. More the sacrifices, it is expected, more will be the inflow of funds from the grantors. More the association of the selfless people with the entity, more will be benefitted the hapless people through enjoying the services, emanating from such organization. Accounting for HRs of these entities, the author thinks, will help the grantor to have information to these ends. A list of other ratios (as mentioned in Chapter Six) like return on investment, margin ratio, turnover ratio, operating ratio, efficiency ratio and various assets turnover ratios[17] will provide sufficient and useful information to the interested parties to have an insight into the welfare activities of a NPO.

The study does not discard the traditional accounting system (though it may appear to be so) rather it aims to provide such information which the traditional system usually does not provide. The study, does not aspire to provide a system which may compete with the traditional accounting system. On the other hand, the suggested system may be used as a supplement to the existing one to make the information system complete, more informative and useful.

We should, however, be cautious about the subjectivity in the estimates presented in the statement. Maximum efforts should be given to formulate the measurement technique so that the scope of personal judgement in measuring the variables in the model will be minimised.

The study cannot be claimed to be a full proof one. It is a humble attempt to find out whether it is possible to provide additional information to measure and report how far the goal of an entity has been achieved. The accounting model suggested in the study, if adopted, the author thinks, additional information so derived will be of much use to the various user groups for evaluating the performance of welfare organizations.

Suggestions for Further Investigation

For the purpose of our research work in measuring the value of HRs associated with NPOs, we have considered the voluntary health and welfare organizations, where the number of selfless people and the degree of their dedication are of much importance. A detailed discussion on the value of them to the entity has been made in Chapter Six. Now let us make an attempt to suggest some related areas where further investigation should be persuaded.

(i) The Performance of a voluntary health and welfare organization is very much depended on the collective efforts of the funding agencies, the selfless employees and the organizers. But these organizations come into existence only because of the service motive of the organizers. Once organized, these entities function with the funds provided by the funding agencies and the active participation of the employees. Sacrifices made by the HRs i.e. the selfless employees (the doctors, assistants and wardboys) are considered here. As the organizers are part and parcel of such entities, value of these people to the organization should also be represented in the balance sheet to make it perfect and more informative. Research in this direction is warranted.

In profit seeking organizations also values of the employees (both executives and non-executives)[18] alone are measured and shown in the balance sheet. But does it fully portray the human resource assets of the organization ? The value of the organizers (i.e. the Board of Directors) to the entity should also be highlighted in the balance sheet.

(ii) Since application of Lev-Schwartz model requires estimation of its various components[19], the presence of subjectivity in these estimates may frustrate the very objective of the investigation. That is why enquiries to be made how the impact of subjectively in the estimates of the quantum of services, market value of these services, discounting factor and similar items can be minimised.

(iii) Analysis based on data of a single year has some importance. But it would be more useful if inter-period comparison of performances of an individual unit is done. This will help to have an idea about the trend of the activities of welfare organization. Investigation on the direction is most desirable.

(iv) Inter-unit comparison is of much use to have an idea about the relative performance of the organizations. The granting agencies are usually confronted with the dilema as to where they should allocate how much of their funds. Enquiries to this end will provide an idea on the effective use of resource bestowed to the individual units.

(v) NPO does not mean welfare organization alone. It embraces clubs, associations, government institutions, educational institutions. The objectives of all these organizations are not identical. But it is a fact that efficient running of such organization is dependent on the effective and collective participation of the associated people. Hence necessary account similar to Service and Sacrifice Account as designed in the present study should be evolved, so that it may commensurate with the respective objective of the organization. That apart, value of these people to such entity should also be made to make the annual reports complete. Investigation to this end will throw much light in the area.

Studies in these areas are to some extent based on subjective estimates. That may limit the usefulness of the evaluation, but there is no doubt, that provides an indication as to what direction the entity is heading to.

References

1. Vide Chapter - Six.
2. Vide Chapter - Six.
3. Vide Chapter - Five.
4. Vide Chapter - Two.
5. Vide Chapter - Three.
6. Vide Chapter - Four.
7. Vide Chapter - Four.
8. Vide Chapter - Five.
9. Vide Chapter - Five.
10. Vide Chapter - Six.
11. Vide Chapter - Six.
12. Vide Chapter - Six.
13. Vide Chapter - Three.
14. Vide Chapter - Three.
15. Vide Chapter - Six.
16. Vide Chapter - Five.
17. Vide Chapter - Six.
18. The Supplementary Annual Report published by the few Organizations and practised the concept of HRA, shows the value of their HRs, by considering the executives and non-executives of their organizations only.
19. Vide Chapter - Six.

Appendix - I

Rama Krishna Mission Boys' Home, Rahara

A/c. Hospital and Dispensary
Income and Expenditure Account
for the year ended on 31.3.1991

Dr.							Cr.
	Expenditure	Rs.	Rs.		Income	Rs.	Rs.
To	**Establishment pay and allowances**			By	Government grants (Maintenance)		19,700.00
	General Department	30,515.00		"	Donations		7,665.00
	Dental Department	3,000.00					
	Eye Department	2,400.00		"	Excess of expenditure over income		40,020.98
	ENT Department	3,000.00					
	Homeopathy Department	2,400.00					
	Puja allowance	925.00					
	P.F. Contribution	372.00	42,612.00				
"	Electrical Charges		4,957.55				
"	Diet Charges		15,127.50				
"	Washing Charges		238.00				
"	**Medical Expenses**						
	General Department	533.65					
	Homeopathy Department	460.84	994.49				
"	Stationary and Printing		177.30				
"	Travelling Expenses		62.00				
"	Bedding and Clothing		250.00				
"	Audit fees and expenses		235.00				
"	**Repairs, renewals and maintenance**						
	General repairing	111.00					
	Repairs of the building	1,249.44	1,360.44				
"	Postage and Telegram		344.00				
"	Hospital utensils and equipments		487.00				
"	**Miscellaneous expenses**						
	Contingencies (Gen.)	526.25					
	Contingencies (Hom.)	2.20					
	Cleaning & sanitation	12.25	540.70				
			67,385.98				67,385.98

Appendix - II

Rama Krishna Mission Boys' Home, Rahara

Balance Sheet
as on 31.3.1991

Fund and liabilities	Rs.	Rs.	Assets	Rs.	Rs.
Building Fund			**Building Fund**		
As per last balance sheet	34,669.07		As per last balance sheet	30,992.00	
Less : depreciation as per contra	1,549.60	33,119.47	Less : depreciation @ 5%	1,549.60	29,442.40
Furniture and equipment Fund			**Furniture and equipment Fund**		
As per last balance sheet	14,181.38		As per last balance sheet	19,047.00	
Less : depreciation as per contra	1,904.70	12,276.68	Less : depreciation @ 10%	1,904.70	17,142.30
Transfer from R.K. Mission General Fund			**Accumulated Deficit**		
As per last balance sheet	2,94,472.10		As per last balance sheet	2,93,283.55	
Add : during the year	40,020.98	3,34,493.08	Add : Excess of expenditure over income	40,020.98	3,33,304.53
		3,79,889.23			3,79,889.23

Appendix - III

Market Value of services rendered in the various departments of the Charitable dispensary of the RKMBHR during 1990-91

Month	Eye Deptt.			ENT Deptt.			Dental Deptt.			General Deptt.			Total
Month 1	No 2	Rate 3	Amount 4	No 5	Rate 6	Amount 7	No 8	Rate 9	Amount 10	No 11	Rate 12	Amount 13	Amount (Rs.) (4+7+10+13)
April	57	25	1,425	22	30	660	45	25	1,125	57	20	1,140	4,350
May	85	25	2,125	26	30	480	44	25	1,100	78	20	1,560	5,565
June	98	25	2,450	33	30	990	32	25	800	60	20	1,200	5,440
July	71	25	1,775	30	30	900	120	25	3,00	82	20	1,640	7,315
August	165	25	4,125	37	30	1,110	119	25	2,975	54	20	1,080	9,290
September	74	25	1,850	19	30	570	67	25	1,675	30	20	600	4.695
October	36	25	900	22	30	660	19	25	475	54	20	1,080	3,115
November	93	25	2,325	45	30	1,350	88	25	2,200	51	20	1,020	6,895
December	76	25	1,900	31	30	930	35	25	875	45	20	900	4,605
January	51	25	1,275	14	30	120	61	25	1,525	16	20	520	3.740
February	82	25	2,050	22	30	660	20	25	500	32	20	640	3,850
March	7	25	175	5	30	150	40	25	1,000	30	20	600	1,925
Total	895		22,375	306		9,180	690		17,250	599		11,980	60,785

* The rates here are exclusive of bed charges. If the patients want to stay in the nursing homes, they are to pay more than Rs. 100 per day in addition to the above rates. However, in the polyclinics there is no facility of staying.

Appendix - IV

Market Value of service rendered by the hospital of RKMBHR during 1990-91

Month	Alopathy Department			Homeopathy Department			Total Rs. (4+7)
	No. of patients	Rate (Rs.)*	Amount (Rs.)	No. of patients	Rate (Rs.)	Amount (Rs.)	
1	2	3	4	5	6	7	8
April	548	50	27,400	103	15	1,545	28,945
May	579	50	28,950	172	15	2,580	31,530
June	392	50	19,600	170	15	2,550	22,150
July	1,152	50	57,600	151	15	2,265	59,865
August	1,027	50	51,350	179	15	2,685	54,035
September	958	50	47,900	144	15	2,160	50,060
October	596	50	29,800	142	15	2,130	31,930
November	942	50	47,100	257	15	3,855	50,955
December	994	50	49,700	205	15	3,075	52,775
January	674	50	33,700	188	15	2,820	36,520
February	928	90	46,400	124	15	1,860	48,260
March	1,108	50	55,400	196	15	2,940	58,340
Total	9,898		4,94,900	2,031		30,465	5,25,365

* It includes the cost of daily bed charges.

Appendix - V

Token collection received from beneficiaries at charitable unit during 1990-91

					Rs.
Eye Department	...	(895 x Rs. 5)	...		4,475
ENT Department	...	(306 x Rs. 2)	...		612
Dental Department	...	(690 x Rs. 2)	...		1,380
General Department	...	(599 x Rs. 2)	...		1,198
		Total	...	Rs.	7,665

Appendix - VI

Social Service rendered to Society (SS)

Total market value of services rendered (P)		
at Charitable unit (vide Appendix - III)	Rs.	60,785
at hospital (vide Appendix - IV)	Rs.	5,25,365
	Rs.	5.86.150
Less token collection received from beneficiaries at Charitable unit (vide Appendix - V)	Rs.	7,665
	Rs.	5,78,485

Appendix - VIIa

Details of doctors and other staffs of hospital and charitable unit of RKMBHR during 1990-91					
	Name of doctors and other staffs	Age	Category	Hours devoted per week	No. of arrivals in of week (6 days)
Hospital					
A.	**Name of Doctors Alopathy**				
1.	Dr. C.R. Das	52	General	2	Once
2.	Dr. N.M. Ganguly	56	General	6	Regular
3.	Dr. A. Chakraborty	60	General	1	Once
4.	Dr. P. Roynandi	45	General	1	Once
5.	Dr. S. Banerjee	60	General	18	Regular
Homeopathy					
6.	Dr. A. Dev	60	General	3	Twice
7.	Dr. D. Dasmohapatra	38	General	6	Thrice
8.	Dr. A. Das	36	General	3	Twice
B.	**Name of attendants**				
1.	Sri R. Dey	52	–	–	Regular
2.	Sri N.C. Modak	31	–	–	Regular
3.	Sri S. Sahu	35	–	–	Regular
4.	Sri S. Roy	33	–	–	Regular
Charitable Dispensary					
A.	**Name of Doctors**				
1.	Dr. S.K. Basak	40	Eye Specialist	4	Twice
2.	Dr. S. Bishnu	45	ENT Specialist	3	Once
3.	Dr. H.P. Aich	55	Dental Specialist	4	Twice
B.	**Name of attendants**				
1.	Sri M. Bhattacharjee	28	–	–	Regular

Appendix - VIIai

Details of assumptions for calculation of salary

1. A person employed in a Government unit in India received the following pay and allowance per month during 1990-91 as per the Government order (This pay structure is considered in this studies for calculating the market value of services of the doctors and other attendants in RKMBHR) :

Basic Pay	–
Add Dearness Allowance [@ 29% of Basic Pay]	–
Add House Rent Allowance [@ 15% of Basic Pay subject to a maximum of Rs. 800 P.M.]	–
Add Medical Allowance [Fixed]	Rs. 16.70

2. Every doctors and other persons involved in the study generally started their service life at the average age of 25 years and the retirement age is fixed at 65 years (although the Government restricts the age of retirement at 60 years, but it is observed from the practical experience that the older people are much interested to serve these voluntary organizations).

3. The doctors in our study although completed their retirement age as per the Government order continue their services in this organization and given the highest pay scale for calculation of their market value of services. It is also taken into consideration that these persons are still competent enough to treat the patients.

4. It is assumed that none of the doctors receive the non-practising allowance fixed by the Government.

5. The fixed medical allowance is taken at Rs. 17.00 for the benefit of calculation.

6. The basic pay is fixed on the basis of information provided by RKMBHR on the age of doctors and attendants.

Appendix - VIIb

Salary of doctors and attendants
during 1990-91
[As per Government Rule]

Name of doctors / attendants		Age	Basic (Rs.)	D.A. (Rs.)	Medical Allowance (Rs.)	HRA (Rs.)	Total (Rs.)
1.	Dr. C.R. Das	52	4,950.00	1,436.00	17.00	742.00	7,145.00
2.	Dr. N.M. Ganguly	56	5,500.00	1,610.00	17.00	800.00	7,977.00
3.	Dr. A. Chakraborty	60	6,000.00	1,740.00	17.00	800.00	8,557.00
4.	Dr. P. Roy Nandi	45	4,200.00	1,218.00	17.00	630.00	6,065.00
5.	Dr. S. Banerjee	60	6,000.00	1,740.00	17.00	800.00	8,557.00
6.	Dr. A. Dev	60	6,000.00	1,740.00	17.00	800.00	8,557.00
7.	Dr. D. Das Mohapatra	38	3,500.00	1,015.00	17.00	525.00	5,057.00
8.	Dr. A. Das	36	3,300.00	957.00	17.00	495.00	4,769.00
9.	Dr. S.K. Basak	40	4,000.00	1,160.00	17.00	600.00	5,777.00
10.	Dr. S Bishnu	45	4,200.00	1,218.00	17.00	630.00	6,065.00
11.	Dr. H.P. Aich	55	5,400.00	1,566.00	17.00	800.00	7,783.00
1.	Sri R. Dey	52	1,670.00	484.00	17.00	251.00	2,422.00
2.	Sri N.C. Modak	31	1,220.00	354.00	17.00	183.00	1,774.00
3.	Sri S. Sahu	35	1,040.00	302.00	17.00	156.00	1,515.00
4.	Sri S. Roy	33	1,000.00	290.00	17.00	150.00	1,457.00
5.	Sri M. Bhattacharjee	28	1,130.00	328.00	17.00	170.00	1,645.00

Appendix - VII(c)

Calculation showing proportionate remuneration of doctors of RKMBHR (Hospital and Charitable Units)

. The important point here is the effective hours of service that the doctors have rendered in the hospital. Generally, a doctor, who is a full-time employee of a hospital, is supposed to be on duty for 24 hours (i.e. whenever he is required he is to attend the patient in the hospital). But generally a doctor provides services for two days in the outdoor department and the other four days he remains busy with operations and other services within the hospital. But if we consider the effective hours of work a doctor, it will be on average 3 hours. Therefore, the total effective hours in a week of 6 days or 18 hours (taking the minimum effective hours of work) and the total monthly effective hours become 72 hours. A case may be cited as an example based on the information provided by RKMBHR for calculation of proportionate salary of doctors. The remuneration fixed for Dr. C.R. Das is Rs. 7,145.00 p.m. (if employed in any hospital or in any other organization). But here he spends 2 effective hours in a week or in other words provides 8 effective hours of service in a month. The proportionate remuneration of Dr. C.R. Das during the year 1990-91 will be :

$$\frac{\text{Rs. } 7{,}145}{72} \times 8 \times 12 = \text{Rs. } 9{,}527.$$

The same method is followed in respect of calculating the proportionate remuneration of other doctors.

2.	Dr. N.M. Ganguly	= $\frac{\text{Rs. } 7{,}977 \times 24 \times 12}{72}$	=	Rs.	31.908
3.	Dr. A. Chakraborty	= $\frac{\text{Rs. } 8{,}557 \times 4 \times 12}{72}$	=	Rs.	5.705
4.	Dr. P. Roynandi	= $\frac{\text{Rs. } 6{,}065 \times 4 \times 12}{72}$	=	Rs.	4,043
5.	Dr. S. Banerjee	= $\frac{\text{Rs. } 8{,}557 \times 72 \times 12}{72}$	=	Rs.	1,02,684
6.	Dr. A. Dev	= $\frac{\text{Rs. } 8{,}557 \times 12 \times 12}{72}$	=	Rs.	17,114
7.	Dr. D. Das Mohapatra	= $\frac{\text{Rs. } 5{,}057 \times 24 \times 12}{72}$	=	Rs.	20,228
8.	Dr. A. Das	= $\frac{\text{Rs. } 4{,}769 \times 12 \times 12}{72}$	=	Rs.	9.538
9.	Dr. S.K. Basak	= $\frac{\text{Rs. } 5{,}777 \times 16 \times 12}{72}$	=	Rs.	15,405
10.	Dr. S Bishnu	= $\frac{\text{Rs. } 6{,}065 \times 12 \times 12}{72}$	=	Rs.	12,130
11.	Dr. H.P. Aich	= $\frac{\text{Rs. } 7{,}783 \times 16 \times 12}{72}$	=	Rs.	20.755

Appendix - VII(d)

Table showing proportionate remuneration of doctors and attendants of RKMBHR (Hospital & Charitable unit) during 1990-91

	Name of doctors	Hours devoted per week / per month 7 (a)	Market value of equivalent service per month 7 (a)	Proportionate value of service devoted to the organization during the year 7 (a)	
			Rs.	Rs.	
1.	Dr. C.R. Das	2/8	7,145	9,527	
2.	Dr. N.M. Ganguly	6/24	7,977	31,908	
3.	Dr. A. Chakraborty	1/4	8,557	5,705	
4.	Dr. P. Roy Nandi	1/4	6,065	4,043	
5.	Dr. S. Banerjee	18/72	8,557	1,02,684	
6.	Dr. A. Dev	3/12	8,557	17,114	
7.	Dr. D. Das Mohapatra	6/24	5,057	20,228	
8.	Dr. A. Das	3/12	4,769	9,538	
9.	Dr. S.K. Basak	4/16	5,777	15,405	
10.	Dr. S Bishnu	3/12	6,065	12,130	
11.	Dr. H.P. Aich	4/16	7,783	20,755	Rs. 2,49,037

The attendants and wardboys are the full-time employees of Rama Krishna Mission Boys' Home, their yearly salary will be :

1.	Sri R. Dey	Rs.	2,422x12	= 29,064	
2.	Sri N.C. Modak	Rs.	1,774x12	= 21.288	
3.	Sri S. Sahu	Rs.	1,515x12	= 18,180	
4.	Sri S. Roy	Rs.	1,457x12	= 17,484	
5.	Sri M. Bhattacharjee	Rs.	1,645x12	= 19,740	Rs. 1,05,756

Appendix - VIII

Sacrifices made by the Service-minded people (W_2)

		Rs.
Market value of remuneration : (vide Appendix - VIId)		
– to Doctors	..	2,49,037
– to Attendants	..	1,05,756
		3,54,793
Less token payment made to doctors and other staff by the organization (vide Appendix I)	..	42,612
		3,12,181

Appendix - IX

Sacrifices made by the Organization (RKMBHR)

$O = [SS - (D + W_2)]$

		Rs.
Market value of social service generated (P) [(vide Appendix - VI]	..	5,86,150
Less token collection received from beneficiaries (Q) [vide Appendix V]	..	7,665
[SS]	..	5,78,485
Less Sacrifice made by the funding agencies [$D = (G + W_1) - Q$] (Vide Table No. 15]	..	59,721
	..	5,18,764
Less Sacrifices made by the service-minded people (w_2) (vide Appendix - VIII)	..	3,12,181
	..	2,06,583

Appendix - X

Human Resource Value under Lev - Schwartz Model from R.K. Mission Boys' Home

	Name of Doctors and Attendants	Age	No. of years remaining for retirement from RKMBHR	Market value of Services (Vide Appendix VIIb)	Proportionate value of whole-time Service during the year (Vide Appendix VIIc)	Discount factor @ 15% p.a.	Total value (Rs.)
1.	Dr. C.R. Das	52	13	7,145	9,527	5.5832	53,191
2.	Dr. N.N. Ganguly	56	9	7,977	31,908	4.7716	1,52,252
3.	Dr. A. Chakraborty	60	5	8,557	5,705	3.3522	19,124
4.	Dr. P. Roynandi	45	20	6,065	4,043	6.2594	25,307
5.	Dr. S. Banerjee	60	5	8,557	1,02,684	3.3522	.3,44,217
6.	Dr. S.K. Basak	40	25	5,777	15.405	6.4641	99,579
7.	Dr. S. Bishnu	45	20	6,065	12,130	6.2594	75,927
8.	Dr. H.P. Aich	55	10	7,783	20,755	5.0188	1,04,165
9.	Dr. A. Dev	60	5	8,557	17,114	3.3522	57,370
10.	Dr. D. Dasmahapatra	38	27	5,057	20,228	6.5135	1,31,755
11.	Dr. A. Das	36	29	4,769	9,538	6.5509	62,482
							11,25,369
1.	Sri R. Dey	52	13		29,064	5.5832	1,62,270
2.	Sri N.C. Modak	31	34		21,288	6.6091	1,40,695
3.	Sri S. Sahu	35	30		18,180	6.5660	1,19,370
4.	Sri S. Roy	33	32		17,484	6.5906	1,15,230
5.	Sri M. Bhattacharjee	28	37		19,740	6.6288	1,30,852
							6,68,417
			Total Human Resource Value		=	Rs.	17,93,786

Bibliography

1. American Accounting Association (AAA), "Report of the Committee on Human Resource Accounting", **Accounting Review** (Supplement) 1973, Volume XLVIII, pp. 169.

2. American Accounting Association (AAA), "Report of the Committee on Accounting for Human Resources", **Accounting Review** (Supplement, 1974, Volume XLIX).

3. American Accounting Association (AAA), "Report of the Committee on Non-Financial Measures of Effectiveness", **Accounting Review** (Supplement, 1971), pp. 80-163.

4. Amesis & Kargas, "Dealing with advances in Accounting Techniques for Hospitals and other Voluntary Health & Welfare Organization," **Accounts' Desk Handbook** - Ch. 8, Third Edition, 1968 Prentice Hall, Englewood Cliffs, New Jersey 07632, pp. 218-245.

5. Anthony, R. N., **Research Report : Financial Accounting in Nonbusiness Organizations : An Exploratory Study of Conceptual Issues.** (Financial Accounting Standards Board, 1978).

6. Anthony, Robert N. "Making Sense of Nonbusiness Accounting", **Harvard Business Review** (May - June, 1980), pp. 83-93.

7. Anthony, Robert N. "What Nonbusiness Organization Accounting Information Do Users Need ?" **Governmental Finance** (May, 1978) pp. 14-16, 18-20.

8. Attkisson, C.C., W.A. Hargreaves, M.J. Horowitz, J.E. Sorenson, Eds., **Evaluation of Human Service Programs** (New York : Academic Press, 1978).

9. Barber. B., "Some Problems in the Sociology of the Profession", Daedalus (Fall 1963).

10. Backer, Richard E., Valdean C. Lembke and Thomas E. King, "Not for Profit Entities", **Advanced Financial Accounting**, McGraw Hill Book Company, 1986 Ch. 20 & 21. pp 997-1085.

11. Bikki, Jaggi & Hon-shiang Lau, "Towards a Model for Human resource Valuation", **The Accounting Review**, April 1974, pp. 321-329.

12. Blaine, E. and W.T. Stanbury, :Accounting for Human Capital", **Canadian Chartered Accountant**, Jan. 1971.

13. Blickendorfer, Richard and Jane Janey, "Measuring Performance in Nonprofit Organizations", **Nonprofit World** 6 (March-April, 1988) pp. 18-22.

14. Brummet, R.L., Flamholtz, E.G. and Pyle W.C., "Human Resource Management - a challenge for accountants", **Accounting Review**, (Volume - 43, No. 2 April - 1968), pp. 217-230.

15. Brummet, R.L., E.G. Flamholtz and W.C. Pyle (Edition), "Human Resource Accounting : Development and Implementation in Industry," An Arbor : Foundations for Research on Human Behaviour, 1968.

16. Butcher, J.V.C., "Employee Evaluation", **The Accountant** (London), August 6, 1970.

17. Caplan, E.H., and Landekich, S., "Human Resource Accounting": Past, Present and Future", National Association of Accountants, New York, 1974., pp 3-4.

18. Chandra Gyan, Paperman Jacob and Sale Trimothy, "Human Resource Accounting : Is it supported by Economic Theory ?" **Indian Journal of Accounting**, Indian Accounting Association, Varanasi, India June-December, 1980 pp. 43.

19. Chandra Prasanna, **Financial Management Theory and Practice**, "Financial Statement Analysis," Tata McGraw Hill Publishing Co. Ltd., New Delhi, 1990.

20. Chastain, C.E., "Evaluation of Human Resource Accounting", **University of Michigan Business Review**, Jan 1979, Vol. 31.

21. Chilingerian, Jon A., and H. David Sherman, "For-Profit Vs. Nonprofit Hospitals : The Effect of the Profit Motive on the Management of Operations", **Financial Accountability and Management** 3 (Autumn, 1987) pp 283-307.

22. Davidson Sidney, "Fund Accounting - Nonprofit Organizations", **Handbook of Modern Accounting**, McGraw Hill Book Company, 1970.

23. Davidson Sidney, Clyde P. Stickney, James S. Schindler and Roman L. Weil, **Accounting : The Language of Business**, 2nd edition, Thomas Horton and Daughters, Glen Ridge, N.J. 1975.

24. Davidson Sidney & Weil L. Roman, "Human Resource Accounting", **Handbook of Modern Accounting** (2nd Edition) McGraw Hill Book Company, N.J. 1975.

25. Dobbins Richards and Peter Trussell, "The Valuation of Human Resources", **Managerial Finance**, pp 103-117,1974.

26. Drtina, Ralph E. "Measurement Preconditions for Assessing Nonprofit Performance : An Exploratory Study", **Government Accountants Journal** (Summer, 1984) pp 13-19.

27. Eggers, H.C., "The Evaluation of Human Assets", **Management Accounting** (New York) November, 1971.

28. Elkin Robert and Mark Molitor, **Management Indicators in Nonprofit Organizations : Guidelines to selection and Implementation** (New York, Peat Marwick, 1984).

29. Elkin Robert and Darrel J. Vorwaller, ":Evaluating the Effectiveness of Social Services", **Management Controls** (May 1972), pp. 104-111.

30. FASB, Trueblood Report : Objective No. 11, as reported in Ahmed Belkaoui, **Accounting Theory**, Harcourt Brace, Javanovich International Edition, Washington, 1985, p. 179.

31. Financial Accounting Standards Board (FASB), Statement of Financial Accounting Concepts No. 4, "Objectives of Financial Reporting by Nonbusiness Organizations", **Journal of Accountancy** (Dec. 1980).

32. Flamholtz Eric, "A model for Human Resource Valuation : A Stochastic Process with service Reward", **Accounting Review** April, 1971, pp 253-267.

33. Flamholtz Eric, G., "On the use of the Economic Concept of Human Capital in Financial Statement : a Comment, **Accounting Review**, 1971 (January), pp 149-154.

34. Flamholtz, Eric. G. **Human Resource Accounting**, Dickenson Publishing Co., Califf, 1974.

35. Flamholtz, Eric. G., "The Impact of Human Resource Valuation on Management Decisions : A Laboratory Experiment". Accounting, **Organizations and Society**, 1976, pp 153-65.

36. Flamholtz, Eric. G., "Human Resource Accounting : Measuring Positional Replacement Costs". **Human Resource Management**, Spring, 1973, pp 8-16.

37. Flamholtz, Eric. G., (1986), "**Human Resource Accounting : Advances in Concepts, Methods and Applications.** Second Edition, Jossery - Base INC, Sanfrancisco, California.

38. Flamholtz, Eric. G. "Towards a Theory of Human Resource Value in Formal Organization," **The Accounting Review**, Oct. 1972, pp 667-678.

39. Flamholtz. E.G., "Assessing the Validity of a Theory of Human Resource Value : An Exploratory Field Experiment", University of Columbia, 1973.

40. Freeman, R.J., C.D. Shouldm and E.S. Lynn, **Government and Nonprofit Accounting : Theory and Practice**, 1988 (3rd Edition), Englewood Cliffs, N.J. : Prentice Hall.

41. Ghosh, Maheshwari and Goyale, **Studies in Accounting Theory**, Wiley Eastern Limited, New Delhi 1990, p. 490.

42. Glautier, M.W.E., and B. Underdown, "Human Resource Accounting", **Accounting Theory & Practice**, Pitman 1983.

43. Goldsmith, R.W. : **Studies in Income and Wealth**, Vol. 12, NBER, 1950.

44. Granof, M.H., and C.H. Smith, "Accounting and the evaluation of Social Programs : A Comment", **The Accounting Review** (July, 1974) pp 822-825.

45. Gupta, R.K., **Human Resource Accounting, Managerial Implication**, Anmol Publication, New Delhi, 1988.

46. Hayes, R.D. and James A. Miller, "Measuring Production Efficiency in a Not-For-Profit setting", **The Accounting Review** July, 1990, pp 505-519.

47. Hakimian, J.S., and Jones C.H. "Put People on Your Balance Sheet", **Harvard Business Review** Graduate School of Business Administration, Harvard College, Harvard, USA, Jan-Feb, 1967, Vol. 45 No. 1.

48. Henke, Emerson O., **Accounting for Non-profit Organizations**, Wordsworth Publishing Company Inc., Belmont Calif, 1966.

49. Hendriksen E.S., **Accounting Theory**, Richard D. Irwin, 3rd Edition, 1977.

50. Herbert Leo, Killough, N. Larry, Steiss, Walter Allan., **Accounting and Control for Governmental and other Non-business Organization**, McGraw Hill Book Co., Ch. 1,1985.

51. Hermanson, R.H. "Accounting for Human Assets," Occasional Paper NO. 14. Division of Research, Graduate School of Business Administration, Michigan State University, 1964, pp 4-5.

52. Hermanson R.H., et al, "Report of the Committee on Human Resource Accounting", **Accounting Review**, Vol. 48, Sept. 1973.

53. Harzlinger, Regina E., and William S. Krasker, "Measuring the Economic Performance of For-Profit and Nonprofit Organizations", **Research in Governmental and Nonprofit Accounting** 2 (1986), pp. 151-172.

54. Heuchan. L., "Nonprofit Charitable Organizations," 1982, **Statistics of Income Bulletin** (Internal Revenue Service, Winter 1985/86), pp 21-40.

55. Hilgert, C., "Nonprofit Charitable Organizations, 1983", **Statistics of Income Bulletin** (Internal Revenue Service, Spring 1987) pp 31-42.

56. Horngreen & Leer, "Governmental and Industrial Accounting," **Certified Public Accountants**, Topic XI, 3rd edition, Prentice Hall Publication, 1976.

57. Ingram W. Robert, Russel J. Petersen, Susan Work Martin, **Accounting and Financial Reporting for Governmental and Nonprofit Organizations :** Basic Concept, "Governmental Accounting Concept," McGraw-Hill Book Co. Inc., 1991.

58. Khandelwal. N. M., "Management of Human Resources in Public Enterprises", Edited by S. Rabishankar and R. K. Misra, Vision Books, pp. 158-182, 1988.

59. Koch, Bruce S., and Sarah A. Reed. "An Examination of Resource Allocation Decisions by ? Charitable Organizations : An Experiment", Unpublished paper presented at 1987 American Accounting Association Meeting in Cincinnati.

60. Koutsoyiannis. A., Modern Microeconomics. ELBS 1979.

61. Leo. Herbert, Larry N. Killough, Allan Walter Steiss, "Accounting and Control for Government and Other Non- business Organization", **Introduction to Accounting and Control for Governmental and Other Non-business Organization**, Ch. 1 pp. 5-19, McGraw-Hill Book Company, 1985.

62. Lev, Baruch and Schwartz, Aba. "On the Use of Economic Concept of Human Capital in Financial Statements". The Accounting Review, January, 1971, pp 103-112.

63. Levine, Abraham. S., "Cost-Benefit Analysis and Social Welfare Evaluation", **Social Service Review** (June 1968), pp 173-183.

64. Likert, Rensis, "Human Resource Accounting : Building and Assessing Productive Organizations" **Personnel**, May-June 1973.

65. Likert, Rensis, **The Human Organization : Its Management and Value**, McGraw-Hill Book Company, New York, N.Y. 1967, p. 1.

66. Likert, Rensis and D.G. Bowers, "Organization Theory and Human Resource Accounting", **American Psychologist**, Vol. 24, No. 6, June 1969, pp 585-592.

67. Linowes, D.F., "Social Economic Accounting", **The Journal of Accountancy** (November, 1968), pp. 37-42.

68. Lipsey R.G., An Introduction to Positive Economics, ELBS, 1972, p. 230.

69. Lloyd Morey and Glen G. Yankee, "Accounting for Non-Profit Enterprises", **Modern Accounting Theory**, edited by Morton and Becker, pp 464-484, 1953.

70. Lynn, E.S., and R. J. Freeman, **Fund Accounting : Theory and Practice**, 1983 (2nd Edition) Englewood Cliff, N.J. : Prentice Hall.

71. Malik, R.K., "Human Resource Accounting Systems", **The Chartered Accountant**, July 1986, p. 7

72. Marshall Alfred, **Principles of Economics**, Macmillan, London, 8th Edition, 1964.

73. May G. Robert, Gerhard G. Muller and Thomas H. Williams, **A. Brief Introduction to Managerial and Social Uses of Accounting**, Prentice-Hall Publication, Inc. Englewood Cliffs, N. Jersey, 1975.

74. Meigs F. Robert and Walter B. Meigs, **Financial Accounting**, McGraw Hill Book Co. 1989.

75. Morey Lloyd and Glen G. Yankee, "Accounting for Nonprofit Enterprises," **Modern Accounting Theory**, Edited by Morton and Becker, 1953.

76. Myers, M.S. and Flowers, V.S. "Framework of Measuring Human Assets", **California Management Review**, Summer 1974.

77. Organ Pekin, "A Human Resource Value Model for Professional Service Organizations". **The Accounting Review**, Vol. LI, No. 2, April 1976, pp 308.

78. Oleck L. Howard, "Nonprofit Corporations and Associations" - **Organizations, Management and Dissolution**, Englewood Cliffs, N.J. 1958, Prentice Hall, Inc.

79. Pauly Mark, and Michael Redisch, "The Not-For-Profit Hospital as a physicians' Cooperative", **American Economic Review** 63 (March, 1973), pp. 87-99.

80. Porwal, L.S., **Accounting Theory - An Introduction**, Tata McGraw Hill Book Company Ltd., New Delhi, 1986.

81. Pyle, W.C., "Monitoring Human Resources on Line", **Michigan Business Review**, Sept-Oct, 1970.

82. Patti, R., "The New Scientific Management : System Management for social Welfare", **Public Welfare** (Fall 1974).

83. Ramanathan, Kavasseri, V., "Social Responsibility of Human Service Agencies", **Journal of Contemporary Business** (Winter 1977), pp. 31-41.

84. Rao, Prabhakar, D., **Human Resource Accounting**, Inter-India Publications, New Delhi, 1986.

85. Rao Prabhakar D., "Human Resource Accounting, In India", Research Bulletin. The Institute of Cost & Works Accountants of India, Vol. X, NO. 1 & 2, Jan & July 1992.

86. Razek, Joseph R., and Hosch, Gordon A. "**Introduction to Government and Not-for-profit Accounting**" (Englewood Cliffs : prentice Hall, Inc. 1985).

87. Ruggels, R. & N. Ruggels, **National Income Accounts and Income Analysis**, McGraw-Hill Book Co., 1949.

88. Sangeladji, M.A., "A Theory and Empirical Investigation of Human Resource Accounting", Unpublished Dissertation, University of Oklahama, 1975.

89. Sherman, David H., "Interpreting Hospital Performance with Financial Statement Analysis," **The Accounting Review** 61 (July, 1986b), pp. 526-549.

90. Sherman, David, H. "Measurement of Hospital Performance and Implications for Accounting", **Research in Governmental and Nonprofit Accounting** 2 (1986a).

91. Siegal, J., "A Survey of Human Resource Accounting", **The Management Accountant**, May 1968 pp. 186.188

92. Simson, Robert. R. (Jr.) "The Measurement of Human Resources". **The Journal of Accountancy**, Sept. 1971.

93. Sinha, G.C., "Accounting for Human Resource", **Accounting Theory**, Book World, Calcutta, First Edition, 1989.

94. Smsith, G. Stevenson, " Performance Evaluation for Nonprofits : A Tested Method for Judging your Organization's Performance", **Nonprofit World** 6 (January-February, 1988), pp. 24-26.

95. Sorensen, James E., and Hugh D. Grove, "Cost-Outcome and Cot-Effectiveness Analysis : Emerging Nonprofit Performance Evaluation Techniques", **Accounting Review** (July, 1977) pp. 659-675.

96. Statement of Financial Accounting Concepts (SFAC) No. 4: "Objectives of Financial Reporting by Nonbusiness Organization" **Journal of Accountancy**, March 1981.

97. Swansn, G.A. and J.C. Gardner, "Non-For-Profit Accounting and Auditing in the Early Eighteenth Century : Some Archival Evidence", **The Accounting Review**, July 1988, pp 436-447.

98. Taylor P.J. and M.W.E. Glautier, "Accounting Information and Industrial Relations : Social Implications and Cost and Benefit Considerations", **Economic Research Paper**, University College of North Wales, Bangor, 1974.

99. Thirlwall A.P., "Growth and Development with Special Reference to Developing Economics," ELBS, 4th edition, 1989, p. 117.

100. Tomassini, L.A., "Assessing the Impact of Human Resource Accounting : An Experimental Study of Managerial Decision Preference", **The Accounting Review**, AAA, Oct. 1977, pp. 4-14.

101. Tomassini, L.A., "Accounting for Human Resources in Financial Planning and Budgeting", **Managerial Planning**, Mar-April, 1978.

102. Warshauer (Jr.) William Malvern J. Gross (jr.), and Joel W : Meyerson, "Nonprofit Enterprises", **Accountants' Handbook**, (Vol. 2, 6th Edition) edited by Lee J. Seidler, D.R. Carmichael, A. Ronald Press Publication, 1981.

103. Woodruff, Robert L. (Jr.), "Human Resource Accounting", **The Canadian Chartered Accountant**, September, 1970.